HISTORY IN THE TEXT

PURDUE UNIVERSITY MONOGRAPHS
IN ROMANCE LANGUAGES

William M. Whitby, General Editor
Allan H. Pasco, Editor for French
Enrique Caracciolo-Trejo, Editor for Spanish

Volume 3
Sandy Petrey
History in the Text:
"Quatrevingt-Treize" and The French Revolution

SANDY PETREY

HISTORY IN THE TEXT:

"Quatrevingt-Treize" and the French Revolution

AMSTERDAM / JOHN BENJAMINS B. V.

1980

For Dosha

Table of Contents

Acknowledgments

A year's study in Paris, sponsored by a National Endowment for the Humanities Fellowship, generated the idea for *History in the Text* and gave me the time necessary to undertake it. I am pleased to acknowledge the Endowment's support at the beginning of the study it made possible.

Previous criticism of *Quatrevingt-Treize* inspired and guided much of my work. Victor Brombert and Guy Rosa, whose studies stand out in a rich body of critical material, were of particular importance as the ideas expressed here were being formulated.

For critical readings and invaluable comments, I am in debt to Fred Jameson, Joan Stewart, Phil Stewart, and Eleonore Zimmermann. The order of their names is alphabetical, my gratitude to them profound.

Introduction

The purpose of this book is to defend the legitimacy of combining the two nouns in its title, the two names in its subtitle. A certain form of contemporary scholarship would reject any such purpose on the ground that "history" and "text" designate radically incompatible entities whose combination produces a grotesque monstrosity. A text is a self-contained signifying whole. Its communicative power derives solely from the abstract structures which constitute different literary codes, all of which are semiotic entities whose components convey meaning by virtue of purely internal relationships among themselves. Critical analysis must consequently recognize a text's confinement within a closed universe whose closure is inseparable from its ability to mean. Textual messages, like all other kinds, signify through arbitrary conventions no more subject to extrinsic explanation than religious mysteries.

The methodological effect of this theoretical orientation is to rivet attention first on the text itself and second on objects to which a text can be legitimately compared, other messages informed by the same conventions. If our goal is to write a history of American advertising techniques, we do not study the fossil remains of pterodactyls. For analogous reasons, we cannot use knowledge of nonverbal entities to illuminate literary creations. The world of words and the world of things being distinct and disjunctive, the assumption that the latter explains or validates the former is a naive instance of the referential fallacy, whose catastrophic effects on literary criticism have been abundantly demonstrated over the last two decades.

The extent to which texts stand apart from history is apparent in one of Marx's famous introductory statements in *The Eighteenth Brumaire of Louis Bonaparte*: "Men make their own history, but they do not make it just as they please; they do not make it under circumstances chosen by themselves, but under circumstances directly encountered, given and transmitted from the past."[1] There are two components to that statement, both of which unequivocally distinguish historical activity from anything literary texts can represent. First, history is what humans "make," not what they say or write. Material praxis and verbal semiosis are irresolvably *other*. *War and Peace* is not war and peace because what is done in the world and what is written in the text have no necessary or sufficient relation to one another. Second, history is made in "directly encountered" circumstances, not in indirect representations of them. In other terms, history occurs within the universe of referents rather than of signs. For the same reasons that there is no one-to-one correspondence between a word and the thing it names, depiction of a historical event cannot attain epistemological adequacy to the event itself. Although human beings make both texts and history, the two kinds of creation demand different tools, different techniques, and different workshops.

The negatives and distinctions could be indefinitely extended, but the main point is already clear: in the full sense of the two nouns, "history in the text" is an oxymoronic phrase. If for no other reason than the number of pages remaining, however, it is also clear that this book will adopt a meaning of "history" and "text" that allows a single discourse to incorporate the two. It remains important to begin by emphasizing that the discontinuity between textual structures and historical events is such that no single inquiry can comprehensively address both. Self-enclosed and self-enclosing, a text draws readers within itself. Open to an indeterminate future and an influential past, a historical epoch derives intelligibility from outside as well as within. To assert that a unitary study could encompass those orthogonal movements would be to begin from a ludicrously mistaken premise.

Nevertheless, there is a perspective within which history and texts are legitimately comparable, that furnished by ideology. The conceptual framework of general semiotics includes ideology as well as literature, yet ideology is also among the directly encountered circumstances within which history is made. The representations we form of our social situation in the actual world are fully commensurate with literary structures representing imagined situations in a fictional world; both achieve coherence through the internal principles of a signifying system. Even though the differences in degree between ideology and literature are massive, the crucial point is that there are no differences in kind. The events of the Terror in the French Revolution are one thing, the ways human consciousness has articulated them are something else. No matter how misguided it would be to examine Hugo's novel on the Revolution in comparison to the world-historical year its title names, it is both permissible and advisable to consider *Quatrevingt-Treize* as part of the representational tradition in which it insistently places itself, that composed of coherent verbal statements of what happened in 1793.

Emphasis on ideology in fact characterizes most twentieth-century discussion of history and literature. The *locus classicus* for that discussion is Georg Lukács' monumental analysis of realist fiction, particularly his fully developed essay on Balzac's *Les Paysans*. Without pretending to a full summary of Lukács' thought, I would like to examine that essay as one extreme in an important debate over ideological limits on fiction's representational possibilities. For Lukács, successful realist novels present ideology and history in forms which mercilessly display the contradictions between them. Textual expression of ideology stands in direct opposition to textual expression of socio-economic reality; false consciousness announces its own falseness by the position it occupies within the fictional universe. "In his quality of writer," Balzac inexorably refuted the vision to which he was faithful "in his quality of political thinker."[2] He intended that *Les Paysans* present the tragedy of the large aristocratic estate. The novel in fact presents the tragedy of the peasant smallholding destroyed by usurious mortgages held by rapacious bourgeois. Balzac "describes with perfect truthfulness the real economic and social factors which make the victory of the bourgeois group over the [aristocratic] Montcornet group inevitable" (*SER*, p. 30) even though real economic and social factors directly contradict his own understanding of the world.

A lexicon of contradictions—"in spite of," "irrespective of," "against his will"—dominates Lukács' style because it dominates his conception of the *Comédie humaine*'s achievement. Balzac's novels are dual objects. On the one hand, they plead for a return to aristocratic and Catholic principles; on the other, they describe social conditions which make restoration of the Old Regime unthinkable. As a consequence, explicitly ideological statements are patently irrelevant to the universe they supposedly explain. Monarchist sentiments in *Les Paysans* are empty nonsense because the novel "presents in literary form the same essential development of the post-revolutionary smallholding that Marx describes in *The Eighteenth Brumaire*" (*SER*, p. 35).

Vigorous denial of the tenet that historical reality can appear "in literary form" characterizes a more recent position in the debate over ideology's literary status. In *La Révolution du langage poétique*, Julia Kristeva defines literary form itself as antithetical to social truth. Dual objects for Lukács, realist novels are for Kristeva hopelessly unitary. Bourgeois ideology has codified the genre so as to exclude all expressions of bourgeois society's actual nature. Kristeva's argument is that ideological deformation not only dominates the novel but also controls the categories permitting socially acceptable communication of any kind. Utterances are revolutionary only if they transcend grammar, logic, and semantics to adopt the (seeming) incoherence of the poetic language devised by authors like Mallarmé and Joyce, whose verbal inventiveness violently "contests the very principle of the ideological" and in so doing "joins social revolution"[3] as a direct menace to the ruling order. The processes which constitute society also constitute the forms to which it assigns signifying power. "Social" and "symbolic" are synonymous (*RLP*, p. 70), the two most fundamental bases of order are "the logic of language and the principle of the state" (p. 78), and textual refusal of socially installed signifying practices consequently "corresponds to socio-economic change, even to revolution" (p. 14).

Because ideology necessarily tends toward stasis, the free verbal play of modern poetry and the liberating *jouissance* of other artistic practices mounts a most dangerous attack on society's means of perpetuating itself. Artistic and political revolution are part of the same thrust toward dissolution of society; poetic language is "a means of action in the process of social transformation" (*RLP*, p. 613). Traditional literature, on the other hand, is by its very nature a major ally in society's struggle for eternal life. A work which makes coherent statements about a social system is by that very fact accepting the standard of coherence which revolutionary works contest. The realist novel dear to Lukács is for Kristeva an endless repetition of the world's understanding of itself, a dead genre incapable of making a revolutionary statement.

While they agree that ideology deforms authentic human situations, Lukács and Kristeva hold diametrically opposed views on literature's ability to represent history. *La Révolution du langage poétique* holds that a realist novel must violate the rules of its existence as a realist novel if it is to incorporate valid historical statements. The ideology which distorts every socially sanctioned communicative act makes all apparent historical situations in literature actual falsifications of historical situation in general. For Kristeva, the traditional criteria of critical judgement—organic form, thematic coherence, representational integrity, stylistic harmony—are so many variants of a single outrageous lie, the idea that a codified aesthetic structure can enclose a human subject. To assume that an accepted genre can communicate historical truth is to be inherently self-contradictory, for societies do not divulge the means for generating utterances able to state what they are.

Yet there is one aspect of social truth which poetic language is equally incapable of stating: the fact that societies are historical and therefore mutable. While Kristeva addresses the factors which situated the revolution of poetic language in late nineteenth-century France, her conception of the revolution's meaning is and must be radically ahistorical. Revolutionary poetry imparts a sign-making capacity ontogenetically and phylogenetically *prior* to social existence. The nonhistorical peoples described by field anthropologists become essentially identical to citizens of the Third Republic, for anyone at any time may respond to signs for which his society does not authorize responses. What Kristeva calls the semiotic *chora* "on the other side of the social frontier" (*RLP*, p. 77) is on the other side of any social frontier that has ever existed or that could ever exist. As historical specificity is textually unutterable, the universe on which the text opens has no historical identity.

Kristeva advances her theses with admirable rigor, and there is undoubtedly a level on which she is correct to maintain that any closed expressive form sustains ideology's drive for inviolable completeness. Nevertheless, there are major differences among the degrees of success with which novels' formal devices enmesh historical reference. Without assuming that fiction can express unmediated socioeconomic insight, it is still possible to examine the resistance *against* aesthetic completeness introduced when a text assumes historically referential language.

Ideology's purpose is to obscure or emasculate the contradictions that shoot through society, a fact which by itself justifies Kristeva's assertion that a formally cogent representation of social contradictions is an impossibility. Like the insane passions of classical tragedy, social threats appear domesticated by their capacity for articulation within the rigid conventions of literary structure. When a cozily familiar naming system can designate a thing, the thing itself becomes cozily familiar. But what happens if the naming process displays its own impotence to designate the world to which it attempts to refer? If literary form buttresses ideology when it succeeds in assimilating social history, then awkward failures to assimilate demystify ideology by exposing the abyss between set forms of thought and the society they must explain. As a corollary of the thesis that a social novel's readability guarantees its ideological corruption, the presence of *unreadable* elements, of sequences which interrupt or sabotage the textual move toward global coherence, forcefully contest ideological falsification.

The proper focus for sociocriticism is neither the validity of historical reference nor the purity of aesthetic structures but the tension between the two. Lukács' analysis of *Les Paysans* can in fact be considered a first step whose continuation must include recognition that the novel as novel is grossly, achingly incoherent. After laboring more than a decade to force his representation of rural conditions into a fictional space, Balzac remained powerless to complete the project he had set himself. "The imagination, the making faculty are inert, don't move, stretch out like whimsical goats."[4] The novel finally published demonstrates that, at least in this case, Balzac's assessment of his creative powers was unimpeachable. Proceeding from a series of vignettes to a series of notes, from a letter to an outline, *Les Paysans* is less a formal development than a centrifugal decomposition. Social commentary repeatedly develops into aesthetic disingetration.

Works like *Les Paysans* suggest a way to combine the apparently contradictory orientations underlying Lukács' insistence on referential validity and Kristeva's identification of codified structures with ideological falsification. Lukács' contention that *Les Paysans* represents history with "inexorable veracity" and "merciless clarity" should be joined to the inexorable fragmentation and merciless confusion which converted Balzac's creative powers into whimsical goats. The validity of Lukács' assumption that there is a possible coincidence between the laws of literary expression and the laws of social development is in this case not an issue, for *Les Paysans* stridently breaks the laws governing novelistic construction. The operative contradiction is not that between Balzac's intention and his accomplishment but that between his novel's success as social document and failure as fictional form. The act of putting history in the text coincided with the dissipation of the text's integrity as literature.

Its generic deformations make *Les Paysans* a limit-text in the same sense that Mallarmé's works are limit-texts for linguistic expression in general. But the conflicts nakedly exposed in *Les Paysans* are also present in novels that less obviously violate generic standards. It is illegitimate to equate a text's formal orthodoxy *in itself* with simplistically ideological copy making. The correct question is the extent to which orthodox form succeeds or fails in assimilating social situations, the degree of self-denunciation in the enterprise undertaken when literature attempts to incorporate historical reference. *Les Paysans* inscribes in itself its impotence to write of the world outside itself, resoundingly admits its failure to generate a novelistic structure capable of representing rural class struggle. Without reaching that extreme, a fascinating variety of nineteenth-century novels also proclaim the discontinuity between the historical ground of their setting and the formal armature of their textuality.

In *A Future for Astyanax*, which shares the Kristevian thesis that conventional literary form cannot express authentic human experience, Leo Bersani also recognizes the sort of gradation I am arguing for here.

> But the critical judgments passed on society in nineteenth-century fiction are qualified by a form which provides this society with a reassuring myth about itself. The realistic novel gives us an image of social fragmentation contained within the order of significant form—and it thereby suggests that the chaotic fragments are somehow socially viable and morally redeemable. The novel makes aesthetic sense out of social anarchy. . . . The novel welcomes the disparate, it generously gives space to a great variety of experience; but it is essentially an exercise in *containing* the looseness to which it often appears to be casually abandoning itself. And even when novelists seem to become more skeptical about their ability to find a saving form for the disconnected, fragmented lives they represent, they make a last-ditch stand for the redemptive pattern rather than simply abandon the whole pattern-making enterprise. [Bersani's emphasis][5]

Bersani directs his attention primarily to novelistic propagation of an "ideology of the self" which denies the complexities of the human psyche. His approach can nevertheless be employed for a discussion of ideology in general because he readily admits the possibility that novels can implicitly contest their own sense-making power while apparently exercising it with smoothly flowing efficiency. Bersani details the ways Flaubert, for example, exposes the spurious character of the emotional intelligibility imparted by literature within a richly intelligible masterpiece in the literature of the emotions, *Madame Bovary*. Analogously, what appears to be a comprehensive novelistic vehicle for expressing society's historical foundation can dispose its historical allusions so as to manifest in fact its *incapacity* to articulate historical reality. Through the discordances between its representations of the French Revolution and the devices constituting its distinctive style, *Quatrevingt-Treize* effects just this demystifying operation.

As Emile Benveniste has pointed out,[6] the most important analogy between language and society is that both appear *natural* to the human beings they enclose. To members of any given community, there is but one proper way to coexist, and the one proper way to express thoughts is that current within the coexisting group. Other syntactic systems, like other social organizations, appear at best bizarre and at worst inhuman. The conservative force of society's ability to naturalize itself is well known; the eternally valid appearance of the linguistic forms accepted within a historically determined speech community has comparably reactionary impact. Inability to think or speak ourselves as other than what we are is a politically paralyzing impediment to social change. Kristeva's recognition of the parallelism between semiotic and social stasis underlies her insistence on the political significance of poetic revolution, and a political event's ability to signify within received expressive frames almost guarantees its inability to institute new political significance.

One of the most obsessively fascinating aspects of the French Revolution is that the people who made it were at least partially aware that their task was to fabricate different ways to represent their lives while constructing a different world in which to live them. The Revolution's great years are almost an exception to the proviso with which Benveniste qualifies his remarks on the general relationship between society and language, the assertion that there are no specific homologies between a particular society and a particular language. It is true that languages with vastly different structures have been current in similar social systems, as political cataclysms have left languages fundamentally unchanged. Nevertheless, while the Revolution failed to transform French in any basic way, its effect on the language's lexicon and suprasegmental social messages was incalculable. Without approaching the global rejection of grammar and semantics attempted by authors like Mallarmé and Joyce, the French Revolution repeatedly affirmed in practice that given signifying patterns are no more permanent than given social hierarchies. Revolutionary action by conscious agents can and did alter meaning systems as well as political institutions.

The great "birth-death of worlds" between 1792 and 1794 was also the great birth-death of words, an annihilation of previous representational categories joined to annunciation of new names for new realities. An astoundingly short period witnessed the rebaptism of all measurements of space and time, the abolition and invention of a complete administrative and juridical vocabulary, the metamorphosis of the map of France and nearly every geographical division within it, and a radical upheaval in all verbal forms employed for first- and second-person encounters. The Revolution, a momentous process of language acquisition as well as the seizure of state power, consistently sought the means to speak itself while exercising the power to make itself.

The impulse behind the linguistic revolution was a faith in the identity of *praxis* and *lexis*, a conviction that the word becomes flesh and flesh the word. The ideal of equality, for example, might be legally codified, but it could not be implemented until abolition of titles and universal use of the

familiar *tu*. A deputation from the sections presented the Convention with a
petition to that effect in 1793 and, typically, began its arguments by proclaiming the need for an all-encompassing revision of the dictionary: "the
principles of our language must be as dear to us as the laws of our Republic."[7]
Demands for specific verbal transformations often began with a similarly
generalized statement that words and things are a totality whose manipulation
had to be global or ineffectual. "Citizens, when the Revolution is completely
made in things, it is also necessary to make it in words."[8] This equation of
words and things was accepted by the Revolution's enemies, the reactionary
purists who regularly assaulted "those who have renounced being French in
their language as well as in their actions."[9] Such attacks often paid unwitting
tribute to the success of the linguistic policy they were denouncing, as Casanova
illustrated in his diatribe against Léonard Snetlage, author of a remarkable
1795 dictionary defining the new verbal "creations of the French people."
"The French language will become a *patois* that good writers will never use. It
will become the language of the masses (*la langue du peuple*),"[10] wrote
Casanova, in the process articulating the binary opposition *good writers / masses*
whose semantic and social validity was precisely what the Revolution wanted
to eradicate. The verbal forms which had encoded a rigidly hierarchical class
division were to be altered so as to express (and help create) the new reign of
liberty, equality, and fraternity.

The most striking manifestation of the Revolution's belief in the interaction
between words and things is the occasional proclamation that there is no line
of demarcation between them. Examples abound, particularly during self-
conscious attempts to impose a revolutionary vision through altering words and
meanings. Perhaps the most extensive discussions of deliberately revolutionary
language change were those that addressed the new system of weights and
measures and the Revolutionary calendar, semiotic innovations manifesting
humanity's will to control the spatiotemporal givens of its existence. "Meter,"
"gram," and "liter" today seem rather less than patent demonstrations of
poesis, but they were presented to the Convention as the quintessence of verbal
adequacy to the extraverbal universe. The following argument, which buttressed
the claims of those supporting implementation of the metric system, is representative of a whole school of thought in its definition of words, the "miniature
of objects," as direct expressions of the referential entities they name. "To be
successful, words must, if it is possible, recall some one of the properties of the
things they represent. . . . They are so to speak the miniature of objects."[11]
Signification may have been an arbitrary process in the degraded meaning
systems of the Old Regime, but the Revolution set out to assure that its
signs were fully and emphatically motivated.

Designation of time was to be no less inherently meaningful than measurement of space. Fabre d'Eglantine's report on the names given months in the
Revolutionary calendar announced the union of signifier and referent identifying

the Word that is with God. "The result of these denominations is, as I have said, that everyone will, by the mere pronunciation of a month's name, feel perfectly three things and all relationships: the kind of season in which the month falls, the temperature and the state of vegetation."[12] That such a concept of signification is intimately connected to political control is suggested by *sans-culottides*, the name assigned the five days of the year not included in the new calendar's twelve months of thirty days each. The revolutionary class which had erupted into human time also inscribed itself in time's names; the agents who made dates like July 14 and August 10 proclaim political positions rather than divide days from one another possessed and used the power to make all temporal divisions announce that time is history.

Those who effected the Thermidorian reaction against revolutionary creation were at least as convinced of signs' referential impact as their opponents. When the bourgeois leaders of the Directorate sought furiously to convince themselves and the world that historical time had run its course, the rebaptisms of the Year II gave way before a wave of debaptisms. Among the first victims was *sans-culottides*, whose lexical elimination was clearly considered essential to repression of the class it named. "The word *sans-culotte* recalls only too powerfully to the French nation the ferocious and barbarous acts whose victim it was. Far from consecrating it in our festivals, in our calendars, in our astronomical observations, the nation's honor seems to require that it disappear forever from our dictionary."[13]

Fear of the signs that spoke the Revolution far outlasted the Thermidorian period to become one of the characteristic motifs of nineteenth-century French politics. For Buchez and Roux, writing their monumental documentary history of the Revolution four decades after the Terror, the *events* of 1793 were inconsequential compared to the *words* in whose name they occurred.

> It is nothing to know how many violent days the Revolution had and how many funerals those days prepared; it is nothing to know the history of uprisings, insurrections, civil war; in all that, the Revolution in fact shows, so to speak, its natural and exterior parts; it is no longer anything but the drama of human passions. Those who wish to comprehend the Revolution, so as to feel it like its contemporaries themselves, must seek its terrors elsewhere. They are in the words the Revolution created or those to which it gave a new sense, in that language impossible to grasp if one forgets for an instant that it personifies everything it names. Brigands, famine, tocsin, treason, club, guillotine are living personifications. There is a soul and a will in the words Convention, Commune, section, Jacobin, Cordelier; and when come the words revolutionary tribunal and Committee of Public Safety, it seems that terror had previously tried only borrowed forms and that now it appears in its true guise.[14]

The revolutionary lexicon had to "disappear forever from our dictionary" because its words were living embodiments of the truth that humans can make their meaning along with their history.

There is of course an amusing semiotic naiveté in this confusion between signs and referents. The absurdities to which such views could lead are evident both in the revolutionaries' exaggerated concern for symbols in determining *civisme* and in the nineteenth-century bourgeoisie's equally comic horror at efforts to reinstate the revolutionary vocabulary. Yet the debates had an underlying theme that is very far indeed from semiotic naiveté, the unarticulated sensation, gripping the Right as well as the Left, that what the French Revolution accomplished was *unspeakable* in inherited discourse. With all due allowance, this rejection of old signifying practices can be approached through Kristeva's concept of the revolution of poetic language. The French Revolution also assumed that the stultifying ossification of received sign systems precluded radically new statements by converting them into decrepitly old expressions. The Revolution's language was the "inverse of common sense"[15] because it represented what had never made sense before, the possibility of an absolutely new beginning for human beings and their world.

As was often the case, Thomas Carlyle best analyzed his contemporaries' attitudes toward the French Revolution. His discussion of the empty space between what history was understood to be and the subject matter presented historians by the Revolution perfectly captures received rhetoric's powerlessness to encompass revolutionary meaning.

> And now, in a new stage of the business, when History, ceasing to shriek, would try rather to include under her old Forms of speech or speculation this new amazing Thing; that so some accredited scientific Law of Nature might suffice for the unexpected Product of Nature, and History might get to speak of it articulately, and draw inferences and profit from it; in this new stage, History, we must say, babbles and flounders perhaps in a still painfuller manner. . . . It is thus, however, that History, and indeed all human Speech and Reason does yet, what Father Adam began life by doing: strive to *name* the new Things it sees of Nature's producing,—often helplessly enough.
>
> But what if History were to admit, for once, that all the Names and Theorems yet known to her fall short? That this grand Product of Nature was even grand, and new, in that it came not to range itself under old recorded Laws of Nature at all, but to disclose new ones? In that case, History renouncing the pretension to *name* it at present, will *look* honestly at it, and name what she can of it! Any approximation to the right Name has value; were the right Name itself once here, the Thing is known henceforth; the Thing is then ours, and can be dealt with. [Carlyle's emphasis][16]

To summarize the main points of that stunningly rich passage, to name a thing is to know it, possess it, and transmute it into something that can be comfortably dealt with. The French Revolution is unique precisely because it *cannot* be named. "Old forms of speech" become incoherent babblings when they address the "new amazing thing" created by revolution. Moreover, history's incapacity to speak articulately signals a much broader failure, the insufficiency of the "laws of nature," of "all names and theorems," of "all human speech and reason." Because a particular form of rhetoric fails in its object, the house of knowledge itself begins to crumble.

This *negative* effect best identifies the subversive import of the French Revolution's semiotic project. The birth-death of words denounced the constricted impotence of ideology, all of whose names and theorems fell short of the reality they were called to encode. When the natural, eternal, and universal way of expressing meaning reveals its temporal, social, and national limitations, categories of what is true threaten to lose their grip on human consciousness. Defenders of the old order who, like Buchez and Roux, equated the words the Revolution invented with the most terrible atrocities it perpetrated were in a sense correct. Even if they did not personify all they named, those words did name what the language of common sense could not. Their ability to do so was dramatic proof of the supremely revolutionary fact that human agents in historical time can alter the ways people decide what makes sense.

If the Revolution's language recalls Kristeva's arguments in denouncing inherited meaning, it is reminiscent of Lukács in its capacity to evoke for subsequent generations the historically concrete events of the Revolutionary period itself. As the previously quoted remarks against the illogical, ungrammatical, and un-French nature of revolutionary utterances uniformly suggest, the most potent threat posed by the Revolution's signs was that they recalled a world which affirmed them as logical, grammatical, and necessary. They represent the *other*, the truth of deeds as well as words incompatible with bourgeois ideology. The discourse of the lunatic, equally alien to the solid categories and static combinatorial possibilities of received rhetoric, makes no political threat because its referents can be comfortably ignored. The Revolution's language, in contrast, embodies the fact that there was a Revolution, a time when speech that ought to be a negligeable eccentricity expressed a collective will toward, in Carlyle's terms, a historical product not subject to historical laws. The danger is not simply the existence of signs which semiotic standards do not authorize but the reality of a praxis which made dominant semiotic standards inoperative.

Novelistic allusions to the French Revolution consequently possess a peculiar quality unusual if not unique among textual designations of historical conditions. While *referential* in the ordinary sense, they can also constitute an abnormally powerful *semiotic* commentary. Textual incorporation of the lexical items given currency by revolutionary practice potentially assaults the foundational condition of standard textual ontology, confinement within the closed universe of discourse conventions. The text implicitly questions its own semiotic rules when it evokes a signifying process in which meaning is not systemically received but politically created. In the case of the French Revolution, referential language, which always points outside the text, also points beyond what appears to be the semiotic realm itself.

Quatrevingt-Treize fully exploits the potential for a global commentary on language and history offered by its chosen subject. The novel's referential statements constantly allude to the *sans-culottes*' power to impose their own signs and their own sense. The events and words of 1793 become different metonyms for the single message that humans can make a world which ideologically informed signifying systems cannot comprehend. *Quatrevingt-Treize* communicates this message through studiously developed reference to specific conditions best analyzed through the procedures suggested by Lukács' concept of realist fiction, meticulous attention to the historical validity of textual information. But *Quatrevingt-Treize*, a novel in the most hidebound tradition of the genre, is also subject to Kristeva's strictures on the reactionary impact of conventional literary form. As a result, *Quatrevingt-Treize* confirms the very ideology whose constrictions it exposes. This contradiction is ultimately resolved by the triumph of traditional form over historical signification, but the dialectic between the novel's two constitutive elements—the upsurge of history *against* the text—never loses its fascinating presence. Not only does *Quatrevingt-Treize* continually refute its own statements, it ultimately calls into question the conditions of possibility for its statement-making power. The subject of the following pages is a discontinuous and contradictory structure that never ceases to threaten the text whose foundation it supplies.

1

Children Belong with Their Mother

Quatrevingt-Treize is clearly a historical novel in the normal use of the term to designate a work set in a period prior to the author's own. If we consider history more than chronology, however, this work should in fact be classified as *anti*historical. It employs a multitude of codes to convey the single message that human beings must refuse the imperatives put by *historical* existence in order to realize their full *moral* potential. Discussion of that refusal will be facilitated if we restrict the term "historical novel" to works which, regardless of their chronological setting, structurally incorporate a historical situation. The most nearly perfect examples are the great realist texts of the nineteenth century. Balzac's and Stendhal's novels depend for their readability on a specific social environment. They make sense only because of a historically determined condition whose proximity to the time of their composition is of no consequence. They are historical not because they present the past but because they present history.

"Temporal" would be a better adjective for many so-called historical novels, those in the tradition typified by Dumas's depictions of history as a form of high fashion in which styles change without affecting what they clothe. In this tradition, strange fashions can in fact be the most substantive manifestation of situation in time. In direct contrast are realist works which, as Auerbach said of *Le Rouge et le noir*, are "almost incomprehensible without a most accurate and detailed knowledge of the political situation, the social stratification, and the economic circumstances of a perfectly definite historical moment."[1]

Eisenstein defined his texts in opposition to temporal works that usurp the label "historical" to disguise a vision of the world which in fact undermines the very concept of a "perfectly definite historical moment." "Everywhere, in America as in France . . . there are always two lovers together in the foreground, and only the background changes. Today it's the French Revolution, tomorrow it's the Commune, but the characters are always the same, and no one is interested in historical events."[2] In temporal fictions, interest centers on individual psychologies to the exclusion of collective structures, and political events attain textual importance only insofar as they affect personal stories. A setting in the past does not suffice to make a historical text. Far from it.

The great interest of *Quatrevingt-Treize* is its refusal to fit into either the historical or the temporal traditions. The novel is antihistorical precisely because it first encloses characters in a definite historical moment, then extracts them from it, first weaves the codes of the French Revolution into its verbal texture, then rejects the linguistic forms imposed by its own choice of subject. Its theme is that history can never block humanity's access to non-history. It expresses that theme through an extraordinary series of confrontations between the devices associated with historical and temporal generic conventions.

Entitled with the name of the great year of the Great Revolution, *Quatrevingt-Treize* opens with a group of Parisian soldiers on a search-and-destroy mission in a Breton forest. The soldiers are seeking the Vendée rebels whose resistance to the Republic constitutes the Revolution's most serious internal threat. They notice signs of human presence, surround the suspicious spot, and discover not enemy forces but a helpless widow and her three starving children. After convincing themselves that the woman is apolitical, the Parisians adopt the family in the name of the Republic.

The novel then introduces the marquis de Lantenac, an imposing old aristocrat on the way from England to Brittany to weld the various rebel groups into a single army and secure a landing spot for the projected English invasion. Lantenac assumes command of a group of peasants and immediately displays merciless devotion to his cause by massacring some of the Republican soldiers encountered earlier and razing the village which had sheltered them. During the massacre, the Royalists wound the peasant mother and take her children hostage. The first of the novel's three parts ends with a beggar in the smouldering village meditating on Lantenac's ferocity.

Part II introduces Cimourdain, an ardent priest turned ardent revolutionary, who is named the Committee of Public Safety's delegate to the Republican forces in Brittany. Cimourdain's main duty will be to supervise Gauvain, a nobleman committed to the Revolution out of his love for the good, the just, and the true. Gauvain's commitment to those ideals developed from the instruction he received from Cimourdain, the new political delegate, who had once been Gauvain's tutor and who still adores his former pupil. The tutor must now instruct his charge in ruthlessness, however, for Gauvain invariably spoils his many victories by refusing to exterminate the Republic's enemies after defeating them. Cimourdain and Gauvain, embodying the inexorable and the clement sides of the Revolution, debate their opposing principles throughout Part III of the novel. They agree on only one thing: the future good of mankind demands that the savage marquis de Lantenac be destroyed. Lantenac is Gauvain's uncle, but even this tie of blood does not blind the normally merciful Republican to the necessity of eliminating the Republic's most formidable foe.

The possibility of that elimination comes when Lantenac, a small band of supporters, and their three captive children are trapped in a tower of Gauvain and Lantenac's ancestral castle. Despite the Royalists' threat to kill the hostages, the Republicans attack and win the tower. A dying rebel sets fire to the building, and the three children are about to be burned alive as the marquis de Lantenac escapes through a secret tunnel. On emerging into the open, however, the Royalist leader is transfixed by the scream of the children's mother. Despite the certainty that to do so will mean capture and execution, Lantenac returns to save the children.

Gauvain, his entire concept of his enemy overturned by the Royalist's sacrifice of his life and his cause, cannot accept the thought that such nobility should be rewarded by the guillotine. He consequently arranges an escape by taking Lantenac's place in the cell of the condemned. When Cimourdain learns of this treachery, his devotion to revolutionary discipline forces him to order his beloved Gauvain's death on the guillotine. However, while Cimourdain the political agent must order Gauvain's execution, Cimourdain the human being cannot survive it. The delegate of the Committee of Public Safety commits suicide when the blade hits Gauvain's neck, and the novel concludes with the souls of the tragically opposed Republicans flying heavenward.

In terms of Benveniste's fruitful distinction between "story" and "discourse," between the plot itself and the supplementary information communicated with it,[3] the preceding paragraphs of course summarize only the story. On the level of discourse, the text contains a vast amount of historical description which was not mentioned, such as the breathtaking pages on Paris and the Convention in Part II. The function of historical discourse will be discussed later; for the moment, let us draw attention to the curiously flabby function of history in the story as it stands. Part I of *Quatrevingt-Treize* introduces Lantenac and the Royalist forces in Brittany; Part II introduces Cimourdain and the Parisian revolutionaries he represents. The scene is clearly set for a spectacular resolution of the conflict in Part Three, but the novel's final section does not conclude with the end of the conflict between Republican Paris and the Royalist provinces. Quite the contrary, political definitions are inoperative in the final narrative sequence, which shows the Republican general first saving the life of the Royalist general and then being decapitated by his Republican ally.

The irrelevance of historical conflict to the final personal stories is matched by the general stasis of the civil war from the beginning to the end of the novel. If we look at the struggle in the West independently of the personalities who wage it, it becomes apparent that nothing happens in *Quatrevingt-Treize*. Part I opens with the war at a decisive stage. Part III concludes with the war at the same decisive stage. This is unusual even for temporal novels. *Gone with the Wind* may convey the impression that the primary effect of the War

Between the States was to annoy Scarlett O'Hara, but the war indubitably ends. *Quatrevingt-Treize* neither recounts nor suggests the end of the war in which it inserts its characters. If we concur with Greimas and other theoreticians of the subject in defining narrative as a sequence proceeding from a disturbed to a stable situation, then there is no historical narrative in *Quatrevingt-Treize*.

In contrast, the novel's personal narrative presents the standard violation and vindication of a stock situation and, furthermore, runs throughout the text. The latter point is significant. Although Lantenac, Cimourdain, and Gauvain are unquestionably the novel's most fully developed characters, their serial introduction makes it impossible for them to furnish the narrative threads which connect the novel's beginning to its end. The characters who do furnish that connection are the ones who, introduced before any of the historically typical protagonists, also motivate the concluding sequence: the apolitical peasant family, Michelle Fléchard and her three children. As the tale of a political conflict, *Quatrevingt-Treize* is a non-story whose end repeats its beginning: *turning point in the war* → *turning point in the war*. As the tale of family tribulations, it presents a much more satisfactory progression: *children separated from their mother* → *children reunited with their mother.*

The political conflict is historically specific, a phenomenon of the precise year which the novel's title names and in relation to which its protagonists define themselves. Michelle Fléchard and her children are politically anonymous. They belong together by a timeless imperative independent of historical events. Although the family's dissolution is the effect of historical struggle, the important point is that the novel's basic narrative axis is the disruption and reinstitution of a situation which is eternally valid. History threatens the family unit's sanctity, but that sanctity as ultimately reaffirmed is luminously transhistorical. Children belong with their mother regardless of the year when they were born.

Then what distinguishes *Quatrevingt-Treize* from the temporal works which Eisenstein scorned? The Russian filmmaker's precise example of stories to avoid was that of two lovers whose career denigrates historical events. Yet family togetherness is no more pregnant with political significance than the union of a man and a woman in love. If it structures its plot as the timeless tale of maternal impulses, why not classify *Quatrevingt-Treize* with thousands of other trivially chronological novels?

The beginning of an answer to those questions is the striking difference between the textual presence accorded the standard lovers and that which *Quatrevingt-Treize* assigns the Fléchard family, between the peasants' contrasted functions on the levels of story and discourse. Eisenstein refused temporal fictions because they place personal stories in the foreground and relegate history to the background. *Quatrevingt-Treize* reverses that emphasis. The Fléchards' central narrative role does not lead to the extensive delineation reserved for historically typical and conscious characters. Lantenac, Cimourdain, and Gauvain's developed textual presences are inseparable from their developed political consciousnesses. The novel assigns negligible personal and political stature to the characters who unify its narrative; the characters presented as political and personal Titans have subsidiary narrative functions.

Quatrevingt-Treize is antihistorical rather than temporal because it refuses to concentrate the reader's attention on characters who act independently of historical movements. It depicts men committed body and soul to historical struggle and recounts the meaningful events of their lives as effects of their political engagement. When those men are inserted into the ahistorical tale of a family reunion, therefore, they must appear there *against* their political definition. Their narrative function requires that they rise above history and act as if their involvement in the war between Republic and Old Regime were a mistake which they fully renounce. Narrative dominance of an ahistorical story corresponds to the thematic dominance of a moral vision in which historical circumstances are insubstantial wisps.

To appreciate the extent to which their participation in the family story denies the value of their political stories, consider the historical consequences of Lantenac, Gauvain, and Cimourdain's involvement with the mother and children. Lantenac is identified time and again as the monarchy's best hope, the one man who can unify the Vendée rebels, open France to the British forces, and restore the Old Regime. "Son nom avait couru dans l'insurrection vendéenne comme une traînée de poudre, et Lantenac était tout de suite devenu centre."[4] The man bearing that explosive name cannot act as an isolated individual. When he returns to certain death for the sake of three children, he is sacrificing the monarchist cause as well as himself. Gauvain's response is even more vilely treasonous. A general of almost supernatural skill, Gauvain alone can withstand Lantenac and save the Revolution. Yet in order to affirm the nobility of the children's rescue, he both releases the Republic's most dangerous enemy and destroys, in himself, the Republic's most successful defender. With Gauvain removed, only Cimourdain might have the strength to organize the Parisian forces; his suicide opens yet another breach.

The chapter which describes Gauvain's conflict over Lantenac has often been compared—the first time by Hugo himself—to "Tempête sous un crâne," the famous chapter in *Les Misérables* in which the real Jean Valjean decides to abandon his secure disguise in order to save a man mistakenly identified as himself. However, while the two chapters are rhetorically similar, the political implications of Gauvain's dilemma confront him with the necessity of a decision wholly unlike Jean Valjean's. The reformed thief condemns himself to assure the safety of an innocent sheep; the Republican general condemns himself so that the wolf will continue to have free run of the fold. Gauvain's sacrifice will lead inexorably to "la mort d'une foule d'êtres innocents, hommes, femmes, enfants, . . . le recul de la révolution, les villes saccagées, le peuple déchiré" (p. 442). Since "sauver Lantenac, c'était sacrifier la France" (p. 442), and since "tuer Lantenac, c'était tuer la Vendée; tuer la Vendée, c'était sauver la France" (p. 368), Gauvain can consider himself only a traitor and a deserter when he decides to liberate his enemy: "Va, fais les affaires des Anglais. Déserte. Passe à l'ennemi. Sauve Lantenac et trahis la France" (pp. 443-44).

Yet this act of black treachery is also an act of radiant virtue. In performing it, Gauvain is bathed in a superior light (p. 438) which, as he goes toward a traitor's death, seems to emanate from his own godlike self. Not only is his face illuminated (p. 489) but the brightness of dawn radiates from his eyes (p. 481). The deed which history marks as infernal is at the same time divine. Instead of damnation, Gauvain achieves an apotheosis.

The same act thus has opposed meanings, and one of the central ideas of contemporary semiotics is that a single signifying element has two meanings by virtue of two codes. One of the codes in this case is a historical system structured by the oppositions which also name the political conflicts of the French Revolution. The other has a radically different foundation. Gauvain comes to assign meaning by a process which, while making the words of 1793 semantically vacuous, also affirms the majestic plenitude of kinship terms. When Gauvain leaves the Revolution to enter the tale of the Fléchard family, the textual presentation of his decision ceases to divide reality by political categories in order to classify it on the basis of family ties.

Earlier, Gauvain and Lantenac's depictions had emphasized that political definition takes precedence over all other kinds. Lantenac is a Royalist and an uncle, Gauvain a Republican and a nephew. Their political commitments suggest hostility, their family bond affection, and political factors clearly determine their interaction. The two men struggle mightily against one another, vying as to which can swear more strongly to exterminate the other. Lantenac, "ce quasi grand-père," promises to kill Gauvain, "presque un petit-fils," like a dog (p. 255). Gauvain is no less adamant. In a discussion with Cimourdain, he explicitly chooses political over familial allegiances: " 'Mais alors, si tu prends Lantenac, tu lui feras grâce?' 'Non.' . . . 'Mais Lantenac est ton parent.' 'La France est la grande parente' " (p. 286). Gauvain's denial is in harmony with the text's overall assertion that ties of ideology are greater than ties of blood. A series of passages establish stylistic fields whose cumulative effect is to annihilate the normal value of family terms, here shown to be politically and hence semantically void. "[C]'est le petit neveu qui se bat contre le grand-oncle. L'oncle est royaliste, le neveu est patriote. L'oncle commande les blancs, le neveu commande les bleus. Ah! ils ne se feront pas quartier, allez. C'est une guerre à mort" (p. 246). The thrice-repeated kinship terms *oncle* and *neveu* are ineffectual in this passage's development toward its concluding war to the death. The operative words are political terms in historically specific opposition: *royaliste/patriote; bleu/blanc*. Gauvain and Lantenac are enemies not relatives.

But only up to Michelle Fléchard's scream. From then on, not only do Lantenac and Gauvain become allies but the vocabulary of family ties attains unforeseen stylistic stature. No longer is France "la grande parente," for Gauvain sacrifices and betrays France. The family bonds which had been nugatory suddenly become a higher truth than the Revolution, a truth which, by a most perplexing historical judgement indeed, it was the Revolution's task to proclaim: "abolir la féodalité, c'est fonder la famille" (p. 438). Instead of the end of the fatherland's most dangerous enemy, Lantenac's execution comes to mean to Gauvain the distressing loss of a revered ancestor.

> Ce sang qu'il allait répandre—car le laisser verser, c'est le verser soi-même—est-ce que ce n'était pas son sang, à lui Gauvain? Son grand-père était mort, mais son grand-oncle vivait; et ce grand-oncle, c'était le marquis de Lantenac. Est-ce que celui des deux frères qui était dans le tombeau ne se dresserait pas pour empêcher l'autre d'y entrer? . . . Il s'agissait de savoir si, quand Lantenac venait de rentrer dans l'humanité, Gauvain, allait, lui, rentrer dans la famille.
>
> Il s'agissait de savoir si l'oncle et le neveu allaient se rejoindre dans la lumière supérieure. (pp. 437-38)

The profusion of kinship terminology—*sang, grand-père, grand-oncle, frères, famille, oncle, neveu*—and the absence of political words lexically embody the value system motivating Gauvain. Historical meaning disappears before a form of sense making organized by ahistorical categories. Not a Royalist and a Republican but an uncle and a nephew join one another in the superior light.

On the symbolic level, Lantenac is not Gauvain's only relative in *Quatrevingt-Treize*. Cimourdain, the former tutor, is both mother and father to his beloved pupil: mother because "l'esprit allaite; l'intelligence est une mamelle" (p. 142), father by a "profonde paternité spirituelle" that makes him "plus père que le père" (p. 142). As with his natural uncle, Gauvain's bond to his spiritual·parent is threatened by political divisions. In the former tutor and his pupil, "deux formes de la république étaient en présence, la république de la terreur et la république de la clémence . . ." (p. 282).

But death itself does not prevent revalidation of Gauvain and Cimourdain's family ties, as the text's final sentence specifies: "Et ces deux âmes, sœurs tragiques, s'envolèrent ensemble, l'ombre de l'une mêlée à la lumière de l'autre." It is as "sœurs," as members of the same family, that Gauvain and Cimourdain leave the Revolution.

Gauvain's reunion with Cimourdain and Lantenac suggests that the opposition between story and history in *Quatrevingt-Treize* should be taken farther than was done before. Not only do the three political protagonists have accessory roles in an apolitical tale, they are also the principal characters in stories as resolutely ahistorical as the Fléchard family narrative. The plot and subplots of *Quatrevingt-Treize* all display a single narrative axis whose sequence depends for its effectiveness on the supremely nonrevolutionary concept that blood is thicker than water: *family ties broken* → *family ties reestablished*. Furthermore, the Revolution consistently has the villainous narrative function of keeping families apart. The course of the civil war separates the mother from her children as their respective ideologies separate Cimourdain, Gauvain, and Lantenac. A major component of the textual definition of the Revolution in *Quatrevingt-Treize* is its disruption of personal and familial relationships.

Only "a," not "the" major component, however. The Revolution is also represented as the great hope of humanity, the creation in blood and fire of a world where love will reign. By the curious judgement quoted earlier, the same Revolution which destroys family ties also affirms their sacredness. This is the paradox discussed in relation to Gauvain's release of Lantenac: a single signifying unit has contradictory meanings, and such a situation can exist only in the presence of distinct sets of semiotic procedures.

Different semiotic procedures, different ways of encoding and interpreting messages, always manifest different means of representing and understanding existence as a whole. The contradictory values of signifying units in *Quatrevingt-Treize*—the rescue of three children, the salvation of Lantenac, the Revolution itself—therefore embody conflicting philosophical assessments of human duty and purpose. *Quatrevingt-Treize* authorizes two interpretations of its textual elements, one based on the events of 1793, the other transcending all historical situations to radiate eternal truth. That phrasing suggests the hierachy by which the decoding possibilities are to be evaluated: historical understanding is inferior. To attain salvation in *Quatrevingt-Treize* is to rise above the universe of *quatre-vingt-treize*.

Lantenac is charged with answering two questions. (1) "Should I allow three children to be burned alive while their mother watches?" (2) "Should I destroy the political cause to which I have devoted my being?" If he were presented with either of those questions in isolation, Lantenac's response would be a resounding negative; but they are not presented in isolation. To say "no" to one is to say "yes" to the other, and his choice is to refuse his historical duty for the sake of something higher. Gauvain faces a comparably impossible pair. (1) "Should I release the Republic's most dangerous enemy?" (2) "Should I execute the protector of the innocent?" He too choses an answer which transcends 1793. The moral duties of a *chevalier sans peur et sans reproche* anachronistically stand above all those urged, however imperiously, by a revolution in process.

Au-dessus des royautés, au-dessus des révolutions, au-dessus des questions terrestres, il y a l'immense attendrissement de l'âme humaine, la protection due aux faibles par

les forts, le salut dû à ceux qui sont perdus par ceux qui sont sauvés, la paternité
due à tous les enfants par tous les vieillards. (p. 442)

That passage's moral hierarchy sets the human soul over and away from earthly
questions like a nation's form of government. Analogously, its verbal hierarchy
invalidates language grounded in oppositions like that between royalty and
revolution. Lantenac and Gauvain are above all historical conflict, and whatever features distinguish political systems from one another are not pertinent
to their meaning.

For Gauvain, Lantenac's decision to negate the semantic value of political
signs was almost conscious.

Quoi, être un royaliste, prendre une balance, mettre dans un plateau le roi de
France, une monarchie de quinze siècles, les vieilles lois à rétablir, l'antique société
à restaurer, et dans l'autre, trois petits paysans quelconques, et trouver le roi, le
trône, le sceptre et les quinze siècles de monarchie légers pesés à ce poids de trois
innocences. (p. 443)

The image of the scale is especially apposite to the change of code Lantenac
effects. As any English word has meaning by virtue of the oppositions between
it and all other English words, so the key political signs *roi, trône,
sceptre*, and *monarchie* are meaningful by virtue of their opposition to the
signs of the revolutionary regime. And as English words are meaningless in
French, so royalist signs are without substance when political discourse is
abandoned. Lantenac's decision to save the children was a choice to stop
representing his life by a historical code suited for earthly questions.

The Royalist general's acceptance of the higher moral order and of a language
adequate to it is transitory. Gauvain's is permanent. When the Republican
leader goes to offer freedom to the Royalist prisoner, the latter gives a
magnificent speech in defense of his cause. His diatribe both raises the language
of Royalist struggle to memorable heights of eloquence and makes acerbically
comic metalinguistic comments on the Republic's feeble attempts to create its
own language: "ce que nous appelons la boue, vous l'appelez la nation" (p. 449).
The response to this eloquence is silence. As if beyond the stage in which
political discourse of any kind conveyed meaning, Gauvain speaks only the few
syllables required to offer freedom to his uncle. Lantenac has reentered a
historical world and uses language capable of speaking it. Gauvain, in a higher
world, cannot respond in kind. "L'Ancêtre" is the title given to the chapter
containing ten pages which are by far the novel's most compelling defense of
the Old Regime and one of its most compelling political statements of any sort,
and it is as an ancestor rather than an adversary that Gauvain responds to
Lantenac. For those above royalty and revolution, silence is the only answer to
historically grounded utterances.

If Lantenac returns to an inferior system of representation, Cimourdain never acquires any other. The political understanding which is his only way of viewing the world forces him to execute his spiritual son. He subsequently finds himself unable to interpret his condition and therefore removes himself from it. Although he used a different vocabulary, Camus defined suicide as the admission of a semiotic breakdown: "killing yourself amounts to confession. It is confessing that life is too much for you or that *you do not understand it.*" [emphasis added].[5] Lack of understanding is a lack of representational capacity, an inability to devise an expression of what is that can accomplish the quintessential human goal called making sense.

Hugo originally planned to include in *Quatrevingt-Treize* an explanation of Cimourdain's suicide as the response to a moral imperative as strong as the political imperative which forced Gauvain's execution. Two manuscript variants show Cimourdain saying that, while the "law" required that Gauvain die, "justice" demands that he follow his former pupil. The decision not to include any such explanation in the final text and to present the suicide as a stark fact was inspired. Cimourdain does not die because he has alternative means of understanding the world, one structured by political categories such as the laws which vary with time and place (recall that "laws" was one of the words Lantenac perceived as meaningless when he replied to a mother's scream), the other structured by moral ideals like justice which are eternally the same. A prisoner of history, Cimourdain can understand the world in only *one* way, through a representational system marked by historical oppositions. That system is inadequate to his apolitical reaction to Gauvain's death, and he leaves a world without meaning.

Cimourdain's desperately unexplained suicide deserves further comment because it indicates the global failure of historical visions of the world in *Quatrevingt-Treize*. When introduced, the priest was presented as the personification of the great political events occurring around him.

"Cimourdain s'était jeté dans ce vaste renouvellement humain avec logique. . . . cette croissance de tout l'avait vivifié. . . . D'année en année, il avait regardé les événements grandir, et il avait grandi comme eux" (pp. 134-35). Completely rejuvenated by the Revolution, Cimourdain understands the world and himself through its development. Only his love for Gauvain prevents him from being an exclusively political creature, and that love is "caché, mais non éteint, par l'immensité des choses publiques" (p. 143).

This immensity of public things is crucial; no less so is the fact that they do not extinguish private things. At the conclusion of the novel, Cimourdain looks at Gauvain and sees a traitor to the cause. That interpretation reverses the one effected when the tutor was forming his charge's mind and the rigorously egalitarian Cimourdain responded not to Gauvain's political meaning but to his childhood. "Que ne pardonne-t-on pas à un enfant? On lui pardonne d'être seigneur, d'être prince, d'être roi. . . . Il est si petit qu'on lui pardonne d'être grand" (p. 141). The final pun on *petit* and *grand*, the former used in its human and the latter in its political sense, perfectly summarizes Cimourdain's semiotic selection. The lexical triplet *seigneur, prince, roi* has no expressive power in comparison to the single word *enfant*. Public things—public names—do not communicate in the private language of love for a child.

Cimourdain's suicide is the result of adopting a converse representational system in which the names of personal affections cannot communicate. Like all characters in *Quatrevingt-Treize*, Cimourdain must confront a fearful choice: *either* he understands the world as political, in which case words like *enfant* have no meaning, *or* he responds to children and denies the significance of political signs. After condemning Gauvain to death, Cimourdain went to see him for the last time. Finding him asleep, the former tutor looked at his child in such a way that "une mère regardant son nourrisson dormir n'aurait pas un plus tendre et plus inexprimable regard" (p. 470). The maternal imagery, highly charged in this story of a peasant mother's reunion with her children, states Cimourdain's feeling. But another word in the quoted sentence underlines the devastating effect of Cimourdain's political vision. He has committed himself to a representational system in which maternal love is "inexprimable."

For Cimourdain, therefore, private things cannot be articulated. For Gauvain, who made the opposite semiotic choice, public things like civil war do not exist. "Et l'on pouvait dire: Non, la guerre civile n'existe pas, la barbarie n'existe pas, la haine n'existe pas, le crime n'existe pas, les ténèbres n'existent pas; pour dissiper ces spectres, il suffit de cette aurore, l'enfance" (pp. 433-34). What is the language in which it "can be said" that civil war does not exist? That in which childhood is synonymous with dawn, "innocence" in apposition with "toute-puissance" (p. 433), and all historical imperatives are seen to vanish "devant le bleu regard de ceux qui n'ont pas vécu" (p. 433).

The repetition of words like "n'existe pas" illustrates the all-encompassing quality of the text's representational shift. The graphic sequence s—o—n has one meaning in French, another in English, a third in Spanish, and so on. However, the meaning it potentially bears in other semiotic systems vanishes—does not exist—when we identify the system in which it actually appears. Once the hermeneutic choice is made, alternative meanings are no longer pertinent. Similarly, the nefarious political meaning of Lantenac's release is of no consequence after the decision that children have absolute value.

Quatrevingt-Treize can be read as a progressive revelation of children's transcendent significance. Before Michelle Fléchard's scream, characters had made the grievous error of interpreting children within a historical frame. The Royalists assumed the Fléchard family was Republican and took the children hostage. Trapped in the Tourgue, they attempted to make political use of the children by threatening that their defeat would be accompanied by the hostages' deaths. Even Gauvain and the Republicans, although they make (unsuccessful) plans for a rescue, act as if civil war imposes duties higher than those owed to children. While they know that the hostages' deaths could result, they nevertheless attack and conquer. The Royalist who sets the fire intended to burn the Fléchards does so with a speech which definitively asserts that children are political signs. Referring to the imprisoned child king Louis XVII, the monarchist explains his arson by saying that he is responding to Republican interpretation of children as political: "Je venge, sur leurs petits, notre petit à nous, le roi qui est au Temple" (p. 402).

When the mother sees her threatened family, however, Royalists and Republicans stop assimilating children into the discourse which opposes them to each other, recognize that the meaning of a child's blue gaze cannot be expressed in the words for which they are killing and dying, and join to affirm words suited to the majestic truth of that which is above the Revolution. The text concurs. On a stylistic level, the radiance of childish innocence generates a series of words whose sense goes beyond that conveyed by the lexicon of 1793. On the narrative level, the novel which appeared to be about the Vendée rebellion reveals that its subject is the reunion of family members—mothers and children, uncles and nephews, fathers and sons. For stories to be stories, they have to have conclusions. Despite the political circumstances of their beginnings, all the stories of *Quatrevingt-Treize* can conclude only by the double move toward affirming the sanctity of family love and rejecting the demands of historical action. To return to Benveniste's formula, both the story and the discourse of *Quatrevingt-Treize* begin in history and end by moving out of it.

The great merit of *Quatrevingt-Treize* is that it makes this move without presenting the historically formed interpretation as *incorrect*. Rather it is *different*. It is not incorrect to say that the signified of s—o—n is "male child," although that meaning is not pertinent if French is the language in use. Analogously, it is not incorrect to say that Lantenac's return to the children and Gauvain's release of Lantenac have ghastly political meanings. That is a fact which the text repeatedly proclaims. Yet the historical significance of those acts is not pertinent to the signifying network in which they are finally assumed, a network whose concepts are eternal not historical. The text presents the meanings of the French Revolution as simultaneously real and inferior.

Quatrevingt-Treize thus arranges its elements so as to announce that they can and must be interpreted by conventions other than those validated by history. The meaning of any sign—words, people, events—varies according to whether it is or is not inscribed in a historical context. Meaning depends on languages; messages communicate only by virtue of codes. While *Quatrevingt-Treize* depicts with great force the power of historical codes, it also demonstrates that they can be transcended by an interpretive procedure which nullifies the oppositions structuring the language of 1793.

2

Meanwhile the Sun Is Rising

Quatrevingt-Treize gives titles to each of its three parts, all of which are divided into titled books which in turn contain titled chapters. Although the interplay of these titles is always a valuable interpretive key, their relevance to the texts they introduce is sometimes not immediately apparent. The title of the novel's last book, "Féodalité et Révolution," is an instance. Those antithetical social terms consitute the most appropriately historical title given to any of the books in this representation of 1793, but the chapters they name appear at best marginally suited to illustrate the central conflict of the Revolution's great year. "Féodalité et Révolution" begins with Gauvain's release of Lantenac and concludes with his and Cimourdain's death. Its first chapter thus contains the long, powerful defense of feudalism and the monarchy discussed earlier, that which Lantenac gives when Gauvain comes to his cell. But that chapter hardly justifies the *pairing* of "Féodalité et Révolution"; it contains no defense of the second term, for Gauvain remains mute before Lantenac's polemic.

In fact, nothing like the ideological confrontation suggested by the final book's title occurs until the last chapter, which begins narration of Gauvain's execution with a stunning description of the guillotine and the Tourgue, a feudal tower whose juxtaposition with the symbol of the Terror brings into direct contact the Old Regime and the movement whose purpose was to annihilate it. Feudalism and revolution acquire palpable form not in conscious humans but in inert objects. The Tourgue embodies the horror of the past, the guillotine the new horror which will wipe the past from memory.

> Un monstre de pierre faisait pendant au monstre de bois. . . . Dans la Tourgue étaient condensés quinze cents ans, le moyen âge, le vasselage, la glèbe, la féodalité; dans la guillotine une année, 93; et ces douze mois faisaient contre-poids à ces quinze siècles. . . .
>
> D'un côté, la dette; de l'autre, l'échéance. D'un côté, l'inextricable complication gothique . . . le nœud; de l'autre, la hache. . . . Elle [la Tourgue] voyait se dresser devant elle et contre elle, quelque chose—plus que quelque chose—quelqu'un d'aussi horrible qu'elle, la guillotine. . . .
>
> La Tourgue, devant la redoutable apparition, avait on ne sait quoi d'effaré. On eût dit qu'elle avait peur. La monstrueuse masse de granit était majestueuse et

infâme, cette planche avec son triangle était pire. La toute-puissance déchue avait
l'horreur de la toute-puissance nouvelle. L'histoire criminelle considérait l'histoire
justicière. La violence d'autrefois se comparait à la violence d'à present. . . . Hier
frémissait devant Aujourd'hui, la vieille férocité constatait et subissait la nouvelle
épouvante, ce qui n'était plus que le néant ouvrait des yeux d'ombre devant ce qui
était la terreur, et le fantôme regardait le spectre. (pp. 483-86)

I have given such a lengthy quotation not only because the series of antitheses
to which it belongs is a memorable instance of Hugo's verbal mastery but also
in order to illustrate the antitheses' foundation in the nature of historical
time. All oppositions are variations on the single contrast between what
society was and what it is: *moyen âge / 93; toute-puissance déchue / toute-
puissance nouvelle; violence d'autrefois / violence d'à present; Hier / Aujourd'hui;
vieille férocité / nouvelle épouvante; ce qui n'était plus / ce qui était.* By their
antithetical inscription into the text, those oppositions constitute a memorable
instance of the novel's use of rhetoric to embody history's meaning. The
development from past to present appears as the most radical of changes, that
which utterly destroys what used to be and replaces it with its opposite.
History creates worlds in a cataclysm as awesome as the original transformation
of what was without form and void into the heavens and the earth.

Except that, unlike Genesis, this text does not look on creation and see
that it is good. Despite their manifold contrasts, feudal tower and revolutionary
guillotine are identically horrible. Past and present are different worlds, but
violence is constant. The word "histoire" appears in the quoted passage only
with the adjectives "criminelle" and "justicière." The present is the deformed
offspring of the past: "Et la guillotine avait le droit de dire au donjon: 'Je
suis ta fille' " (p. 485). With historical struggle occurring between a stone
monster and a wooden monster, humanity's options are limited to choosing the
mouth by which it wishes to be devoured.

Although the novel's final chapter thus fulfills the promise made by the
title of its final book, to confront the Old Regime and the new world, it does
so in such a way as to plead the necessity of a third choice. What will be is
fouled by what was. Man can change the face of his horror, but he cannot
emerge from it. The possibility of escape—from history as well as horror—
appears when the text suddenly changes codes. The rhetoric of historical
change vanishes and is replaced by the bucolic language of a hymn to nature.

Ce matin-là, jamais le ciel frais du jour n'avait été plus charmant. Un vent
tiède remuait les bruyères, les vapeurs rampaient mollement dans les branchages, la
forêt de Fougères, toute pénétrée de l'haleine qui sort des sources, fumait dans
l'aube comme une vaste cassolette pleine d'encens; le bleu du firmament, la
blancheur des nuées, la claire transparence des eaux, la verdure, cette gamme
harmonieuse qui va de l'aigue-marine à l'émeraude, les groupes d'arbres fraternels,
les nappes d'herbes, les plaines profondes, tout avait cette pureté qui est l'éternel
conseil de la nature à l'homme. (p. 486)

The contrast between this writing and the preceding description of a world-historical confrontation is staggering. Rhetoric organized by antitheses disappears before a verbal symphony in which differences exist only as separate notes of a single harmonious scale. Instead of horror, there is charm; instead of being placed in symbolic battle, objects are fraternal; instead of the dogs of war, there are the birds of peace. The distinction between old and new becomes inconsequential beside the infinitely greater contrast between *any* activity in time and the purity which is "l'*éternel* conseil de la nature." Human deeds are social deeds; whatever distinguishes their various forms is meaningless beside the transcendent "contraste de la beauté divine avec la laideur sociale" (p. 486). As when Michelle Fléchard screamed, historical oppositions cease to signify and the representation of another world begins.

In the final sentence of the antithetical series, the guillotine and the tower abruptly appear not as the embodiment of vast social forces but as insubstantial illusions, less embodiments than disembodiments: "et le *fantôme* regardait le *spectre*." That clause ends the historical code in more ways than one. It proclaims the incorporeal status of any historical signs in the nature code which immediately follows it, language as inadequate to representing human action in the world as it is ideally adapted to representing God's music in the trees.

"Spectre," the word chosen to conclude the historical rhetoric, had appeared earlier in a perfectly homologous context. When Gauvain recognized that Lantenac's rescue of the children meant that civil war in particular and revolutionary action in general do not exist, that action was also designated as a "spectre," one dissipated by "cette aurore, l'enfance" (p. 434). In the present instance, the dissipation remains implicit, but its textual manifestation is identical. A prose style marked by the oppositions which structure the language of historical conflict vanishes to be replaced by a style in which history is inexpressible.

Historical signs are spectral and, like ghosts, they vanish with the dawn. Earlier, the metaphoric dawn of childhood made civil war disappear. Here the actual dawn of a new day disperses feudalism and revolution. The title of the novel's final chapter is "Cependant le soleil se lève," meanwhile the sun is rising. The final book, "Féodalité et Révolution," thus begins with a chapter whose title, "L'Ancêtre," suggests family ties and ends with a chapter whose title names the eternally recurring cycle of a bright sun and blue skies. Moreover, the text of the final chapter introduces the language of history only to abandon it for the lyricism which speaks the fresh smell of a warm morning.

In the double meaning of "meanwhile" and "nevertheless," "*Cependant* le soleil se lève" suggests the relationship between history and eternity communicated throughout *Quatrevingt-Treize*. Guillotine and feudal tower acquire awesome verbal intensity, but *meanwhile* the sun is rising and the air smells sweet. The struggle of historical forces is about to cause Gauvain to die, but *nevertheless* the language of Romantic nature ecstasy is pertinent to the text's concerns. While the Revolution is real and requires special writing, the apolitical world of mothers, children, flowers, and springs is no less real and no less imperious in demanding its own language. Different discourse forms alternately affirm history and deny it.

The novel which heaps together sociohistorically charged words like "le fisc, les gabelles, la mainmorte, les capitations, les exécutions, les prérogatives, les fanatismes, le privilège royal de banqueroute, le sceptre, le trône, le bonplaisir, le droit divin" (p. 484) follows them with "le bleu du firmament, la blancheur des nuées, la claire transparence des eaux" (p. 486). A text's choice of styles encodes its vision of the world. By devices like its frequent use of referential language and rhetorical forms whose effect is inseparable from a sense of historical time, *Quatrevingt-Treize* presents the world as the creature of conscious human activity whose most explosive species is revolution. By devices like adoption of the vocabulary of Romantic poetry and narration of idyllic relationships, the same novel declares that the world is, meanwhile and nevertheless, the stage for an eternally recurring cycle of seasons, dawns, births, and loves whose meaning is impervious to collective action at a definite historical moment. Revolution and springtime appear in distinct verbal forms, so arranged as to make the latter an escape from the former.

Hermeneutic difficulties, for characters and readers, arise when signifying units are decoded through inappropriate interpretive conventions. If the pertinent code is not applied, then signs either receive an incorrect sense or appear as senseless as an Egyptian hieroglyph or a Hebrew character in a language which uses the Roman alphabet. The novel's final chapter opens with an astounding commentary on just such hermeneutic errors. In nature language, the political sign formed by the guillotine is alien and nonsignifying, a foreign element whose status is precisely that of an Egyptian hieroglyph or a Hebrew character.

> Le jour ne tarda pas à poindre à l'horizon.
> En même temps que le jour, une chose étrange, immobile, surprenante, et que les oiseaux du ciel ne connaissaient pas, apparut sur le plateau de la Tourgue, au-dessus de la forêt des Fougères.
> Cela avait été mis là dans la nuit. C'était dressé, plutôt que bâti. De loin sur l'horizon c'était une silhouette faite de lignes droites et dures ayant l'aspect d'une lettre hébraïque ou d'un de ces hiéroglyphes d'Egypte qui faisaient partie de l'alphabet de l'antique énigme.
> Au premier abord, l'idée que cette chose éveillait était l'idée de l'inutile. Elle était là parmi les bruyères en fleur. On se demandait à quoi cela pouvait servir. Puis on sentait venir un frisson. (p. 481)

That description of nature violated is also astute metalinguistic commentary. Not only does the text say that "les oiseaux du ciel ne connaissaient pas" the guillotine, it explains their failure to understand the sign as failure to recognize a language, using in the process concepts close to Saussure's fundamental division of the sign into signifier and signified. Like the linguistic units of the antique enigma, the guillotine is not a formless, meaningless *object* but a *signifier*, something known to convey meaning even if not an identifiable one. This sign is strange and surprising, but it is in no way senseless. Its signified ("l'idée que cette chose éveillait," a prophetic formulation indeed) is originally not conveyed only because the historical code determining it does not seem applicable when the guillotine is against the horizon, its blade "noir sur l'azur du matin" (p. 482). The blue horizon ought to be the backdrop for nature's eternally returning goodness rather than for human beings making their history. There among the flowering heather, the guillotine is a semiotic interloper.

The shudder accompanying recognition of the guillotine's sense is the effect of recognition that the historical code is after all applicable. "En même temps que le jour" and its pastoral language, the text introduces a contradictory set of signs. The way is prepared for the long confrontation between the guillotine and the Tourgue. The rhetoric of that confrontation does not, however, abolish the knowledge that meanwhile the sun is rising. "A mesure que le jour montait, l'ombre portée de la guillotine décroissait sur l'herbe" (p. 487). When the text ultimately reverts to the idyllic code of blue sky and green grass, historical signs appear only as static to be drowned out as the tower and the guillotine are drowned in dawn.

> [T]out avait cette pureté qui est l'éternel conseil de la nature à l'homme. Au milieu de tout cela s'étalait l'affreuse impudeur humaine; au milieu de tout cela apparaissaient la forteresse et l'échafaud, la guerre et le supplice, les deux figures de l'âge sanguinaire et de la minute sanglante; la chouette de la nuit du passé et la chauve-souris du crépuscule de l'avenir. En présence de la création fleurie, embaumée, aimante et charmante, le ciel splendide inondait d'aurore la Tourgue et la guillotine, et semblait dire aux hommes: Regardez ce que je fais et ce que vous faites.
> Tels sont les formidables usages que le soleil fait de sa lumière. (pp. 486-87)

The text's stylistic disposition repeats the sky's command. It offers a choice between language representing "la création fleurie, embaumée, aimante et charmante" and language grounded in "l'âge sanguinaire et la minute sanglante." The options are darkness or light, horror or beauty, what men do in history or what nature does in eternity.

The final chapter thus repeats the semiotic shift which accompanied description of Gauvain's decision to release Lantenac, again alternating distinct systems for understanding and representing the world. Those systems can be contrasted either in long passages like those above or in succinct nonsequiturs like this: "On voyait sur l'estrade de la guillotine le bourreau qui allait et venait. La clarté grandissante du matin emplissait majestueusement le ciel" (p. 488). Those two sentences have the same referent but give it radically different meanings. One vision is marked by an executioner and a guillotine, the other by majestic morning light. Gauvain, although about to die at the hands of the executioner, has clearly chosen to represent his world through the second vision, in which the guillotine does not exist: "il dédaigna la guillotine" (p. 489).

The sun, which also scorns the guillotine, appears to recognize that Gauvain speaks its language. It shines on him as on one of its own. "Le soleil, l'enveloppant, le mettait comme dans une gloire" (p. 490). So illuminated, Gauvain is the opposing pole of two contrasts. First, he is opposed to Cimourdain who, still caught in history, stands as black as the guillotine against the blue sky (p. 488). Second, *gloire*, here naming Gauvain's radiance, had just appeared as the synonym of shame, and its negative meaning was the effect of its place in a historical code. The Parisian soldiers, watching the preparations for the death of their chief, were confusedly remembering victories over the forces of reaction. Although they had formerly thought that they were winning the fight for a new world, "il leur semblait maintenant que toute cette gloire leur tournait en honte" (p. 488). History is transient, nature forever. *Gloire* defined by historical action is a sign that can become its antonym; defined by eternity, it has the same sense until the sun grows cold. All that remains before absolute perfection is for death to eliminate even the appearance that Gauvain exists in time.

Commentators on *Quatrevingt-Treize* have generally recognized the supremacy of transhistorical virtues in the moral hierarchy it establishes. But they have also tended to assume that this hierarchy includes a place for the Revolution, that validation of eternal virtues does not denigrate but sanctifies the movement attempting to forge a society where men can live by them. The morally luminous Gauvain is after all a deeply committed Republican leader who chooses last words that affirm his ideological faith, "Vive la République!" Do not such utterances ground the novel's moral vision in historical movements essential to whatever value morality has?

Not at all. Gauvain dies hailing a republic incommensurable with any that could be created by the conflict between Old Regime and new order. Gauvain himself recognized that there is no time and no place for the republic he foresees. It cannot exist in France, for he chose to labor for it by betraying France. "J'ai oublié la France livrée à l'Angleterre; j'ai mis en liberté le meurtrier de la ·patrie" (p. 462). It cannot exist in history, for history is conscious action by conscious agents against opposition. Gauvain's republic refuses both components of that definition, human events and human conflict. In the code of moral certainty assumed by Gauvain, "events" is a sign as meaningless as a guillotine among the flowering heather: "que me font les événements, si j'ai ma conscience!" (p. 479). Human beings do not make this republic by choosing its form and giving it a content. They attain it either through a natural process like old trees' replacement of young ones (p. 477) or by rising in mystical progress on the "échelons de l'échelle qui monte à Dieu. . . . Quand on est au haut de l'échelle, on est arrivé à Dieu. Dieu s'ouvre; on n'a plus qu'à entrer" (p. 476). With God in charge, humanity's motto is not *faire* but *laisser faire*: "'Il y a quelqu'un qu'il faut toujours laisser faire.' 'Qui?' demanda Cimourdain. Gauvain leva le doigt au-dessus de sa tête" (p. 479).

Gauvain's Platonic language (the ladder that rises to God) describes a Platonic concept, a republic whose everlasting beauty and truth are impervious to the disputes characterizing historical existence. To attain truth involves no more agitation than to contemplate beauty. Creation of Gauvain's republic requires neither expropriating the expropriators nor correcting any other injustice; men need only learn to use what a beneficent nature has given them (p. 475). Gauvain has reached timeless enlightenment, a state so removed from humanity's condition that it takes away his breath as well as his voice: "il semblait qu'il ne respirait plus, tant il était attentif à ce qu'il voyait sous la voûte visionnaire de son cerveau" (p. 480). When Cimourdain accused him of being "en plein songe," Gauvain responded that that was the same as being "en pleine réalité" (p. 475). That is in a sense correct, for Cimourdain's reality, historical struggle for historical goals, no longer exists for Gauvain now that his reality is purely internal.

It might be objected here that Gauvain twice repeats a phrase which proves that, far from removing himself from time, he is acting so that time may come to have meaning. When, during his discussion with Cimourdain, Gauvain lapses into silence and smiles beatifically, he tells Cimourdain that he is thinking about the future (p. 481). "Je pense à l'avenir" is repeated in the description of Gauvain mounting the guillotine steps (p. 489). *Avenir* surely implies a commitment to history, a struggle in time to make what will be, better than what is.

But *avenir*, like all key items in the lexicon of *Quatrevingt-Treize*, has different meanings according to the code in which it appears. After his ascent, Gauvain's representation of the world does not include a future which human action can create, which a society in process can model. Since he is about to die, his own future is definitive separation from the world of time, freedom from the contradictions of history and the burden of matter. His future republic is equally immaterial.

The distinction between a historical future and that which Gauvain envisions is apparent if we compare the enlightened one's "je pense à l'avenir" to an earlier description of another man awaiting the guillotine: "Ça m'ennuie de mourir. J'aurais voulu voir la suite" (p. 190). Gallows humor about a desire to know what will be instead of saintly contemplation of what always is— Gauvain's *avenir* has nothing to do with this *suite*, which conveys the contingencies of historical struggle rather than the certainty of eternal peace.

Gauvain's execution is a symbolic as well as an actual transcendence of history. First he removes the marks of his political identity, his commander's sword and scarf, thus completing the process begun when he gave away the cape of a Republican general so that the Royalist general could escape. This stripping away of one set of identifying marks is matched by receipt of another. Gauvain becomes a "vision" (p. 490) whose matrix is nature not society. His long hair floats in the wind, and in the passage discussed above, the sun encloses him to itself. Gauvain dies a historical death for politically damnable treachery, but he simultaneously acquires eternal life in sunlight and innocence.

The double meaning of Gauvain's death is the final instance of the two interpretive systems validated by *Quatrevingt-Treize* and of the text's failure to resolve the contradictions it introduces. Gauvain remains a traitor although he is also a son of the morning. In the end, the assertion that the sun rises despite everything fails to dissipate the imperatives of world-historical struggle, less of a spectre than might be wished. For a discussion of history in the text, however, this failure to be univocal is in itself testimony to the power of *Quatrevingt-Treize*. Historical meaning acquires a textual presence so compelling that the attempt to void it necessarily fails. The Revolution was a collective decision to transform the universe and to create a language worthy of a new world. The novel presents that decision as leading to conditions so bloody that the sun turns away from them, but history remains visible despite the protagonist's decision not to look at what the sun refuses to see. The language of history does not go away despite the text's assertion that it conveys no real significance. The material possibility of a *suite* does not vanish in the radiance of a spiritual *avenir*.

The final pages' transcendence of historical codes includes an intriguing variant on one of the text's basic semantic oppositions which demonstrates that the novel must wrench itself out of what it was in order to make history meaningless. From its beginning, *Quatreingt-Treize* defines the Revolution as the unhappy union of two components, one "political," the other "human." Those two words roughly designate actions taken *against* definite groups of people and actions taken *for* all mankind. "La ténébreuse loi des suspects" (p. 124) typifies political actions, universal education human actions (p. 202). The substance of these two categories is problematic although their differential status is pellucid. To use one of the novel's favorite images, political and human deeds can no more be confused than light and darkness (pp. 202, 208). Their certain opposition even makes possible the moral-historical arithmetic in judgements like this: "Des onze mille deux cent dix décrets qui sont sortis de la Convention, un tiers a un but politique, les deux tiers ont un but humain" (p. 203).

In essence, Gauvain's release of Lantenac allowed him to rise from the political to the human, to cease defining himself against historical enemies and to begin to reply to categories like children and the family, which signify to all mankind for all time. In his discussion with Cimourdain, Gauvain uses a variant to the political/human contrast to express the distinction between the Revolution's present and his future: "chaque siècle fera son œuvre, aujourd'hui civique, demain humaine" (p. 477).

As the antithetical description of the Tourgue and the guillotine makes clear, however, the attempt to create a human world imprisons men in the old politics. Gauvain's silent smile is a confession that there is no language for the human meaning he thinks he understands. A comparable problem was apparent in the novel's depiction of the Convention, which guillotined as well as devised the metric system. The resounding voice that spoke the eternal words justice, tolerance, goodness, truth, love (p. 202) is the cracked voice whose words passed quickly and disappeared forever: "Court et terrible souffle des bouches humaines!" (p. 200). Revolutionary words were both transitory because bloody and eternal because good. The dilemma is how to reconcile these contradictory characteristics of any historical speech.

There is of course no reconciliation possible, so the text is constrained to abandon history altogether. Gauvain avoids the impure speech of humans in process by keeping silent, the novel by abolishing the positive value it had attached to the word *humain*. Earlier the Revolution had, however awkwardly, been both good and evil. In the final chapter, it is wholly evil. As Gauvain loses all the marks of his condition as a human agent acting in time, the term formerly used to laud the worth of one aspect of human activity comes to excoriate the foulness of them all. *Humain*, instead of being opposed to what is political and bad, is now contrasted to what is natural and good. Nature crushes man under the contrast between divine beauty and social ugliness (p. 486). The text crushes the reader under the contrast between the words *humain* can modify and those it cannot. *L'abomination humaine, la difformité des lois humaines*, and *l'affreuse impudeur humaine* are juxtaposed with *douceur universelle* and *éblouissement éternel* (p. 486). Humanity, time, and space are trivial in the semantic field of nature, eternity, and universality.

Homme fares no better than *humain*. Like the adjective, the noun is marked as negative by both the words with which it appears and those to which it is contrasted. "L'homme brise et broie, l'homme stérilise, l'homme tue; l'été reste l'été, le lys reste le lys, l'astre reste l'astre." (p. 486). History is change, and only what remains the same is acceptable. Stars, lilies, and summers are eternally pure, revolutions vilely historical. The final chapter's reversal of the sense previously accorded human terms is the admission of a failure to incorporate historical and moral values into a single representation of the world.

Eternal and historical forms of discourse finally appear irresolvably Other. Jerkily alternating sequences of natural and historical language are the formal equivalent of a thematic organization in which characters cannot struggle for a political program at the same time as they devote themselves to moral excellence, in which Lantenac and Gauvain betray their parties for the love of children. The text finally conflates revolutionary guillotine and feudal castle into a single non-sense. What communicates is the poetic presentation of a beautiful morning in God's country, where humans do not act and things do not change. Feudalism and revolution assault one another, but meanwhile and nevertheless the sun is rising. Revolutions bring convulsive upheavals in time and space, but nature offers the stasis of things which, like the words that name them, are always and ever identical to themselves: "l'été reste l'été, le lys reste le lys, l'astre reste l'astre."

The final preference of natural stasis over historical dynamics is analogous to the transformation effected when what seemed to be a story about the course of civil war resolved itself into the tale of how families belong together. The basic structures of *Quatrevingt-Treize* all display the same organization. History appears to create new ways for humanity to give itself meaning, but this appearance is illusory. Armies and nations come and go; mother love and Mother Nature remain.

The novel's first and last sentences encapsulate its verbal development:

> Dans les derniers jours de mai 1793, un des bataillons parisiens amenés en Bretagne par Santerre fouillait le redoutable bois de la Saudraie en Astillé.

> Et ces deux âmes, sœurs tragiques, s'envolèrent ensemble, l'ombre de l'une mêlée à la lumière de l'autre.

Quatrevingt-Treize opens with insistently referential language. We are in 1793, a date whose extratextual meaning also structures the fundamental opposition of the sentence it introduces, that between "parisiens" and "Bretagne." Those toponymics, concretely situated in time as well as in space, set the tone for the text which follows through a historically created significance summarizing the struggle of the Old Regime against the new society. In stark contrast, *Quatrevingt-Treize* concludes with a sentence in which referential language is impossible, one whose *actants* are not historically specific human agents but spiritually ennobled human souls. Accordingly, the last sentence's fundamental opposition is the eternal contrast of light and shadow rather than the historically determined struggle between two regions. The text of *Quatrevingt-Treize* assumes an axis which proceeds from one form of discourse to its opposite in a verbal development which perfectly complements its thematic organization.

3

Pastoral and Historical Discourse:
Some Absolutes Are More Absolute than Others

The stylistic opposition between the first and last sentences of *Quatrevingt-Treize* remains to be defined on a theoretical level. The most efficient means of doing so is to apply a crucial distinction in twentieth-century linguistics, one grounded in the recognition that stable, homogeneous, structured, and ordered language allows communication among people whose experiences are shifting, diverse, heterogeneous, and unstructured. Any member of a speech community knows both the uniquely personal episodes of his or her own biography and the systems of social conventions which transcend individual variations and thus permit all members of the community to understand messages in the same way. For example, the kinds of food consumed by speakers of English is as unimaginably varied as the manner of their consumption. That does not prevent the signifier *food* from conveying a single signified. Appeals to diverse experience are clearly useless in efforts to state what the common signified is. Meanings are nodal points in the differential structure by which the English language assigns signification to all its lexical items. Only the abstract structure itself, never the concrete biographies of individual speakers, permits the English lexicon to mean.

The distinction between a person's knowledge of chaotic experiences and his simultaneous knowledge of an organized structure is sometimes metaphorically expressed as that between a mental dictionary and a mental encyclopedia. My mental encyclopedia may store any amount of autobiographical information with the signifier "dog": memories of early morning walks in the cold or of a long wet tongue in the face, concern with the rising cost of meat byproducts, satisfaction at the thought of the dog's pleasure when I come home at the end of the day, and so on. However, none of this information figures in my mental *dictionary* which, like those of all English speakers, attaches only abstract semantic features like animateness and four-leggedness to "dog."

Although used by linguists to designate the distinction between individual memories and social semantics, the dictionary/encyclopedia contrast also applies to a central concern of contemporary literary criticism, the referentiality problem. Realist discourse includes much language identical to that found precisely in encyclopedias, where words are used to convey exact historical and geographical information about something other than words. On the other hand, the almost universally accepted concept of a text as an inherently unified "verbal construct in which meaning is achieved by reference from words to words, not to things,"[1] depends on the resources furnished by the mental dictionary's storage of information which language itself attaches to lexical items. A literary text works because it plays on the elements within the competence of anyone able to read the language in which it is written. Its meaning is independent of its capacity to evoke individual experience or extratextual knowledge. Literature signifies by activating different components of the only resource it possesses, certain words in a certain sequence and the codes in which they figure. Its signifying matrix is what has always already been spoken and written, not what has been done in the philosophical construct sometimes called the world.

How do texts *appear* to refer to the world? By judiciously choosing signifiers whose form identifies them as belonging to the corpus of words seemingly able to designate specific parts of reality. Michael Riffaterre convincingly demonstrated that this is to some extent the case when, at the Cerisy colloquium on teaching literature, he rewrote a page from *La Débâcle* by substituting toponyms taken from the Landes telephone directory for the names of villages around Sedan which actually appeared in Zola's text. The change is unnoticeable; Riffaterre's version conveys the same impression of meticulous accuracy as Zola's. Signifiers of the form "X-Village" or "Y-les-Forges" appear geographically precise although in fact they are not, thus justifying Riffaterre's conclusion that "alteration of reference to the real did not threaten mimesis of the real."[2] Abstract marks actually included in our mental dictionary create the false impression that the text is making encyclopedic reference to an extralinguistic universe.

The corpus markers borne by lexical items are pertinent to the verbal demarcation of distinct forms of discourse in *Quatrevingt-Treize*. Let the first and last sentences again serve as examples.

> Dans les derniers jours de mai 1793, un des bataillons parisiens amenés en Bretagne par Santerre fouillait le redoutable bois de la Saudraie en Astillé.

> Et ces deux âmes, sœurs tragiques, s'envolèrent ensemble, l'ombre de l'une mêlée à la lumière de l'autre.

In the first sentence, graphic forms signal encyclopedic designation of precise referents' situation in time and space. Beginning with a date whose numerical form identifies it as temporal specification regardless of the reader's knowledge of what happened in the year it names, the text continues with a series of personal names and toponyms—*Bretagne, parisien, Santerre, Astillé, Saudraie*—which, again independently of our knowledge of the people and places they designate, achieve mimetic intensity through visual features like capitalization. The opening sentence furthermore identifies a military situation by words like *bataillons* and *fouillait le redoutable bois*, whose martial significance defines the novel's subject even for readers who have never heard of the Vendée rebellion.

The verbal characteristics of the last sentence could not be more different. Not only are all graphic marks of situation in time and space absent, but the sentence's lexical constituents are either like *âmes* in admitting no perceptible referent in the world or like *sœurs, ombre*, and *lumière* in proclaiming their signification to be metaphorical rather than referential. Both sentences are of course nothing but words, yet they are crucially distinct in that the last one tells us so.

For Tzvetan Todorov, fantastic literature characteristically induces uncertainty about whether the world it describes is governed by physical laws. Fantastic language is distinct from superficially similar fantastic metaphors in poetry because the question of whether poetry represents a physical world never arises. "If it is said, for example, that the 'poetic I' flies away into the air (*s'envole dans les airs*), it is only a verbal sequence, to be taken as such without trying to go beyond the words."[3] There is a happy coincidence in the fact that Todorov's example and the last sentence of *Quatrevingt-Treize* both have *s'envoler* as main verb, for Todorov's remarks apply perfectly to Hugo's conclusion. The novel begins with a temporal prepositional phrase which introduces a profusion of lexical items apparently pointing away from themselves toward the world. It ends with a sentence in which a canticlelike *Et* introduces words so emblazoned with self-referentiality that any effort to go beyond them is unthinkable.

The central tenet of structuralist criticism is the brilliantly simple fact that verbal phenomena have a verbal cause. It is not the events of 1793, the conflict between two forms of government in a theater in the west of France, which distinguishes historical discourse in *Quatrevingt-Treize*. Rather a certain form of signifiers is disposed in a certain way to produce comparable reactions in readers through the manner in which their mental dictionaries store linguistic information. The wealth or poverty of a particular reader's mental encyclopedia is in theory not functional in his response to the text.

Unhappily, the theory is manifestly inadequate. It cannot begin to explain the contrast between the Parisian/Brittany and light/shadow oppositions discussed above, for example. The last sentence does in fact evoke exclusively the abstract signifieds of *ombre* and *lumière* by using them so as to preclude the possibility of their being taken to designate something in the world. But the first sentence's opposition between Paris and Brittany is not semantically but historically grounded. It exists only because of the conditions prevailing in 1793, when men like Santerre devoted themselves to a specific form of historical activity. Without the encyclopedic knowledge which groups the first sentence's *1793, Santerre, parisiens,* and *Bretagne* in a single conceptual field, the text's opening sentence would not mean what it means.

The verbal nature of verbal phenomena is a self-evident truth. But we must not allow it to hide the fact that words signify regardless of our ability to explain how. Although the problem of where the signifying power of proper names comes from is theoretically unresolved, that power certainly exists. Contemporary models of mental dictionaries are incapable of explaining what distinguishes Hugo's opening sentence from a transformed version like this: "In the last days of May, 763, one of the Aixois battalions brought into Québec by Pétain was searching the awesome Bois de Boulogne in Martinique." To forestall a possible objection, that transformation preserves the syntactic positioning and the French morphology of the original. The point of the new version can perhaps be made clearer by suggesting an entirely different sentence: "After the success of his coup on 18th Brumaire, Ethelred the Unready, despite strong Falangist opposition, ordered that the Unification Church's rites be followed in all Carthage's think tanks."

Although they violate no canons inscribed in the mental dictionary, such as that which forbids taking literally a human's statement that he is flying into the air, those two imaginary sentences proclaim themselves to be exactly what Todorov characterized poetic metaphors as being, purely verbal sequences that repel all efforts to make them anything else. The crucial point for consideration of history in the text is that the formal marks which distinguish between signifiers in the two forms of discourse developed by *Quatrevingt-Treize* are *not sufficient* to define their opposition. In addition to those features that identify a lexical corpus, historical discourse in Hugo's novel assigns words the signification they possessed during the French Revolution. Referential ignorance of the hostility between Paris and Brittany is as great an impediment to understanding Hugo's introductory sentence as semantic ignorance of the antonymic relationship between light and shadow is to understanding his conclusion.

In addition to proper names, the text often plays on the historical resonance of common words. To take some of the more obvious examples, *terreur, citoyen, bleu, patrie, révolution, guillotine, prêtre,* or *guerre* convey much more than can be explained by their abstract semantic features. They figure forcefully in a body of language which never ceases to make explicit and implicit appeals to the reader's knowledge of the events of the French Revolution.

Since a text is nothing but words in sequence, it goes without saying that its analysis must always be linguistically based. But there are major areas of verbal meaning which contemporary linguistics has thus far been unable to address convincingly, and among them is the entire area of referential coherence that is our present concern. I know of no serious effort to describe the semantic content and combinatorial restrictions of proper names like "Waterloo" or "Watergate," nor am I aware of any theory capable of explaining in formal linguistic terms what distinguishes referentially chaotic sentences like those given above from referentially precise utterances like the sentences which begin *Quatrevingt-Treize*. Excluding mental encyclopedias from speakers' linguistic competence was an axiomatic step of immense heuristic value, but it has led to models of mental dictionaries which are inherently unable to describe the full meaning of texts like *Quatrevingt-Treize*.

There are three possible ways of dealing with that inadequacy. The first is to attempt to eliminate it by elaborating a new model for linguistic analysis. I am not qualified even to begin such a task. The second is to follow the example of critics who pretend that there is no inadequacy and attempt to show that the only features which distinguish referential language from other kinds are purely formal. While the discussion above hopefully demonstrates that I believe this supposition has a great deal of merit, it also contains a great deal of silliness. Its effect on practical criticism has often been to produce tortuous demonstrations of what is already known. These demonstrations are classic instances of the "discovery procedures" for which the transformational grammarians ridiculed Bloomfieldian linguists and whose nefarious effects on literary criticism Culler's *Structuralist Poetics* has amply demonstrated.

The third course, the one adopted here, is to admit that this theoretical inadequacy exists and proceed as if it did not. The fundamental assumptions of this analysis are that referential information and verbal features interact throughout *Quatrevingt-Treize* and that their interaction is ultimately responsible for both the novel's global coherence and its communicative force. A discussion of Hugo's title can serve to illustrate this interaction.

Let us first adopt the discovery procedures imposed by a critical approach which denies that referential information is pertinent to decoding a text and assume we know nothing about *quatrevingt-treize* other than the fact that it names a number. The novel's first sentence immediately specifies that this is a special kind of number by identifying it as a designation of 1793, a year whose ominous meaning is apparent in the martial language it introduces. Following that opening, the text repeatedly underscores the awesome force of its titular number by placing it in the semantic field of belligerent and criminal terms. Furthermore, "93" also appears in several identity statements which further magnify it by equating it with semantically charged nouns: "93 est la guerre de l'Europe contre la France et de la France contre Paris. . . . 93 est une année intense. L'orage est là dans toute sa colère et dans toute sa grandeur (p. 135).

Those two quotations both begin paragraphs, a positioning which highlights the fact that sentence-initial numerals preclude normal capitalization. This graphic strangeness is consonant with the fact that Hugo's title is (as he insisted it must be) misspelled. The correct form is *quatre-vingt-treize*, not *quatrevingt-treize*. That distortion inscribes in the signifier something of the effect the text attributes to the referent, an effect in turn consonant with the title's intertext. The name of the Revolution's great year was something of a mystical symbol for the nineteenth century, which often used it as a vehicle for meaning all the more important because it could not be precisely stated. Two of Hugo's poems are typical of his age's magnification of the number he chose as his title.

> Dans l'histoire où tu luis comme en une fournaise,
> Reste seul à jamais, Titan quatrevingt-treize!
> Rien d'aussi grand que toi ne viendrait après toi. ("Nox")

> Quiconque t'osera regarder fixement,
> Convention, cratère, Etna, gouffre fumant,
> Quiconque plongera la fourche dans ta braise,
> Quiconque sondera ce puits: Quatrevingt-treize,
> Sentira se cabrer et s'enfuir son esprit. ("L'Echafaud")[4]

Through appeals to this kind of intertext and to the graphic forms and stylistic fields established in the text itself, rigorously verbal criticism could cogently and productively address words like Hugo's title. The preceding discussion does not depend on any extralinguistic information, and it nevertheless defines the major textual functions assumed by *quatrevingt-treize* and its substitutes.

Yet there are two convincing objections to such an analysis. First, like all discovery procedures, it is open to the criticism that it discovers what was known in advance, that the choice of pertinent semantic fields from this and other works is possible only because of the historical knowledge supposedly being bracketed. Second, no purely verbal procedure can explain the *effect* of the semiotic upheaval brought about by the title's graphic form and identification with words such as *guerre* or *orage*. This is by far the more important point. The text's definition of *quatrevingt-treize* is not just a semiotic exercise. It is also philosophical commentary on the impact of human action as manifested in human representational systems.

One of criticism's most valuable borrowings from Saussurean linguistics is the concept that meanings are "purely differential and defined not by their positive content but negatively by their relations with the other terms of the system. Their most precise characteristic is in being what the others are not."[5] This principle means that the literary text communicates through what it does *not* say as surely as through what it says. To borrow a common formulation no less expressive for being paradoxical, the text achieves its meaning through the presence of what is absent. If we apply this concept to the title of Hugo's novel, it is apparent that its graphic distortion and semantic turbulence are more striking because '93 is not permitted to attain the tranquil status of the number it is.

You know where you are with numbers. With a fixed place in a frozen series, they constitute a reassuringly static corpus that permits no alteration under penalty of reduction to meaninglessness. For all time, 93 comes after 92 and before 94. Like Roquentin's circle, it is not absurd; because, like

Roquentin's circle, it does not exist. *Quatrevingt-treize*, however, names some-thing that does exist. Accordingly, it refuses the semiotic status of a number. Human action occurred, a name was given to it, and then the name violently threw off the lexical properties it had formerly borne. It is just such a relation between verbal features and historical dynamics that underlies the intensity of the representation of the French Revolution in *Quatrevingt-Treize*. The novel contains a massive number of semiotic deformations developing from the progression effected when the neutral number of the title becomes the name of a world-historical year in the first sentence. The signs which permute *in* the text are those that name historical forces *outside* the text. In other words, one pole of the fundamental stylistic opposition in *Quatrevingt-Treize* is marked both by vacillating signification and historical reference.

The assertion that a text is composed of nothing but language, which is a form not a substance, is true but trivial. Although it is the fundamental presupposition of practical criticism, it cannot by itself inform any critical inquiry worth undertaking. The task of criticism is first to make explicit the text's use of semiotic identities and differences and then to define the global meaning produced by the particular signifying process under discussion. Con-sidered purely as signs, *quatrevingt-treize*, the guillotine in the flowering heather, and Gauvain and Lantenac's sacrifices have in common pronounced indeterminacy. Their sense depends on the form of language which incorporates them. One set of meanings is grounded in the violent social transformation that created the politics of modern France, the other in purely verbal constructs. It would be foolish to pretend that this commonality is a bizarre coincidence which does not function in the reader's decoding of the novel.

Quatrevingt-Treize constantly accords dates syntactic and semantic properties incompatible with their ordinary grammatical status. As 1793 *is* war instead of the time for war, so months and days are removed from their normal verbal environments.

> Le 14 juillet avait détruit.
> Le 10 août avait foudroyé.
> Le 21 septembre fonda. (p. 179)

The paragraphing of those three sentences, each reduced to the minimal grammaticality of noun phrase plus verb, effectively foregrounds the noun phrases' peculiarity. They have left the corpus of modifiers and become agentives. Names of revolutionary *journées* designate not neutral chronology but violently creative history; their syntactic status in Hugo's text manifests disruption of the world through disruption of representational forms.

Throughout the novel, dates have comparably perverse grammatical functions often emphasized by the paragraphing in the above quotation. For example, in one scene Danton defends himself against Marat by proclaiming his inclusion in another date series: "J'étais du 14 juillet. . . . J'étais du 6 octobre. . . . J'étais du 20 juin. . . . J'ai fait le 10 août" (p. 164). Any explanation of the novel's verbal structure would have to confront this systematic use of temporal modifiers to name historical events, and the conclusion of the discussion has to be that the text's use of time markers ultimately redefines time itself. To name a date is to state that men acted on it.

Again the important point is that the verbal configuration which establishes abnormal semantic and syntactic functions has an extraverbal foundation. *Quatrevingt-Treize* employs not just any dates but the great days of the French Revolution in its identification of time with history. The novel's coherence depends on the referential association of this particular device with all other historical signs. Historical discourse is a style of writing characterized by two inseparable features; in this text, the words which refer to the events, participants, and dates of the French Revolution are the words which assume peculiar stylistic functions whose analysis requires suspending all preconceptions about the grammatical configurations a given lexical corpus can assume. Referential specificity and verbal instability mark a single stylistic procedure. Historical discourse simultaneously points beyond the text and points up the instability of words within it.

On the other hand, stability is the most prominent characteristic of the other form of discourse in *Quatrevingt-Treize*, that in which "l'été reste l'été, le lys reste le lys, l'astre reste l'astre" (p. 486). Such tautological assertions that A = A are in context far less pointless than they appear, for they are in direct contrast to a form of language in which A ≠ A, September 21 does not remain September 21, and 93 is distinct from 93. Before discussing this second form of discourse, it may be advisable to eliminate a possible misunderstanding. Because of the blatantly referential resonance of isolated signs like "1793," the preceding discussion has for brevity's sake addressed them as if they had inherent meaning. That is of course not the case. A message communicates only by virtue of a code, and to alter the code is to alter the meaning any sign conveys. Dates no more have a given historical character than lilies have a given ahistorical character. The objects of inquiry are global configurations not individual words, and the text can of course alter any word by placing it in another configuration. Even the most highly charged historical sign can be presented so that its historical resonance is muted. To retain the example of dates, consider the following sentences.

Tous les rois ont senti sur leurs nuques le 21 janvier. (p. 190)

Le 21 janvier, pendant que la tête de la monarchie tombait sur la place de la Révolution, Bézard, représentant de l'Oise, allait voir un tableau de Rubens trouvé dans un galetas de la rue Saint-Lazare. (pp. 196-97)

Both sentences include the element *21 janvier.* But only in the first does the date display the characteristics of historical signs outlined above—substitution of the time when action occurred for the name of the action itself, assumption of the reader's referential knowledge of what that action accomplished, and correspondingly unusual grammatical functions. Our mental encyclopedia can explain how *21 janvier* can denote something perceptible on the napes of kings' necks. Our mental dictionaries cannot. In the second quotation, none of this applies. *Le 21 janvier* gives the temporal setting for an explicitly stated action; it takes the normal position for an adverbial phrase; and the historical event which occurred on the date is not assumed but stated. The second sentence describes a man removing himself from history to contemplate the eternal beauty of art. The form of description includes a sign analogously separated from the historical signification it had borne a few pages earlier.

What is true of historical discourse in *Quatrevingt-Treize* is also true of its opposite: the implication that certain signs are inherently vested with a certain meaning is a shorthand which can be adopted only if we presuppose the truth that signs are individually meaningless. That being said, let us proceed to the signs most consistently opposed to those identifying historical discourse, as in the final chapter's juxtaposition of language naming castles and guillotines with language rotating around dawns and summers. The basic dichotomy is between nature and history, each of which generates a distinctive lexicon and syntax to impose its own set of interpretive procedures.

The other opposition previously discussed is that between the apparent chronicle of a civil war and the actual tale of children's needs. Here, too, one pole of the opposition is history. In place of the expected story line organized by sociohistorical development, the reader finds a series of plots structured by the reestablishement of family ties. This narrative organization is so independent of a society in historical process that its conclusion requires the disappearance of its actors from the text although the historical tales in which they also appear remain achingly incomplete. Once the Fléchard family is reunited, no further mention is made of them despite their involvement with an army at war. When Gauvain comes back into the family and releases Lantenac, the uncle vanishes from the novel. When Gauvain and Cimourdain are joined in death, the Revolution which had separated them loses all claim to textual consideration, and the novel closes with no hint of the future outcome of the war.

Historical chronicle is thus opposed to family narrative as historical discourse is opposed to nature language. Their common opposition unites nature and children in a combination which alludes directly to a particular literary genre, the pastoral. As it has developed from the ancients, the pastoral vision has consistently expressed an *alternative*, a way of life different from that furnished by society as it is. The genre began when Theocritus wrote poems about Sicily and Cos as a refusal of the Alexandria in which he was living, and its persistence through subsequent millenia derived in large part from the otherness of its subjects. To the corrupt foulness of artificial men and the cities they had built was opposed the tranquil simplicity of a bucolic world and the natural beings it nourished. Pastoral's stylized descriptions of nature, essential to the genre, delimit a universe in which people form a continuum with the birds of the air and the beasts of the field.

In the nineteenth century, pastoral underwent a fundamental transformation. The escape offered by a natural setting, by another world, began to be replaced by memory of an innocent childhood, of another time. Empson's superb essay on the version of pastoral in Lewis Carroll's Alice books explored the pastoral tradition's "shift onto the child."[6] Following Empson, several critics have addressed the analogy between shepherds living in nature and children living in innocence.

> Ultimately, therefore, the dominant idea of pastoral is a search for simplicity away from a complexity represented either by a specific location . . . from which the refuge is a rural retreat to Arcadia; or from a specific period of individual human existence (adulthood) from which the refuge is in the vision of childhood.[7]

Quatrevingt-Treize asserts the pastoral identity of children and nature in a series of passages reminiscent of imagery prominent in the contemporaneous *Art d'être grand-père*. The third book of the novel's third part, for example, describes the Fléchard children in language that consistently portrays them as being as much a part of nature as the archetypal shepherd and shepherdess. A young girl's foot is so like the dawn that "il eût été difficile de dire quel était le plus rose" (p. 328); a bee flies into the children's room as if to say, "J'arrive, je viens de voir les roses, maintenant je viens voir les enfants" (p. 335). When the young peasants are awake, they speak the language of the birds: "Ce qu'un oiseau chante, un enfant le jase. C'est le même hymne" (p. 328). The children's sleep is "l'affaire de l'univers . . . les feuilles ne bruissaient pas, les herbes ne frissonnaient pas. Il semblait que le vaste monde étoilé retînt sa respiration pour ne point troubler ces trois humbles dormeurs angéliques. . ." (p. 347). Equation of God's children with God's country began with the family's introduction in a wood that fed, housed, and protected them. It continues until their removal from the novel.

While *Quatrevingt-Treize*'s allusions to pastoral are thus generically orthodox in their assimilation of nature and children, the novel also includes a critical variant on pastoral conventions, for here the pastoral world's separation is not complete. Arcadia can become an ideological battleground in which children are victims instead of exemplars. Rather than the possibility of withdrawal from a world that is too much with us, *Quatrevingt-Treize* offers a way to reinterpret the world which does away with the "too much" while preserving the "with us." Pastoral discourse in this novel communicates a different way of representing the world, not a different world. Dramatic alteration of meaning occurs through a series of revelations that what appeared to demand historical representation can in fact be depicted in the discourse of pastoral.

Refusal of history has always figured prominently among pastoral's constituents, but the standard refusal involves representing a universe from which history is absent. In *Quatrevingt-Treize*, it is present but (potentially) meaningless. As the Tourgue and the guillotine are "drowned in dawn" when the text chooses to look at what the sky does instead of at what men do, so depiction of children repels the signs of historical conflict dominating the universe outside. Military commands like a repeated "Attack!" do not penetrate the Fléchards' playroom, another space where it "can be said" that civil war does not exist. In the final chapter, the sun's ascent dissolves the cacophony of feudalism and revolution into the "harmonious scale" of natural music. An identical metamorphosis takes place when the children listen to the grating noises of impending battle and perceive them as a "kind of harmony" sounded by God:

> [D]es chevaux hennissaient, des tambours battaient, des caissons roulaient, des chaînes s'entreheurtaient, des sonneries militaires s'appelaient et se répondaient, confusion de bruits farouches qui en se mêlant devenaient une sorte d'harmonie: les enfants écoutaient, charmés.
> —C'est le mondieu qui fait ça, dit René Jean. (p. 336)

That passage's development is paradigmatic of the representational shifts made in *Quatrevingt-Treize*. The world does not change, but its meaning is altered beyond measure.

Pastoral imposes the concept of cyclical time, of an eternally recurring series of events whose existence and order are guaranteed by the nature of things. History imposes the concept of linear time, of a contingent series of events which can transform, definitively and cataclysmically, the nature of things. Two texts which abundantly illustrate these contradictory senses of time are the Convention's Revolutionary calendar and Spenser's *Shepheardes Calander*. The former typifies the Revolution's iconoclastic semiotics. The signs it invented assert that humanity is the ruler and hence the namer of the universe. Time, declared to have begun again with the foundation of the Republic, was henceforth to be measured in units made by and for those who had seized ownership of history. Weeks, days, and hours were divided into units of ten. Even the cycles of the moon were not perceived as a given fact which humanity was constrained to accept; debate centered for a time on ways to give the year ten months so that it too could manifest the number of digits on the hands that were molding their world.[8] Although the decision was finally to leave the moon as it was, the twelve months were made to proclaim their historical status by new names and new definitions. With each month having thirty days, the five days remaining at the end of the year were to become national festivals, the *sans-culottides*. Those festival days were consecrated to activities worthy of the revolutionary class whose name they bore. During the festival of opinion, for instance, citizens were encouraged to express with impunity whatever they thought of any public official at every level. From Jefferson to Mao, revolutionaries have been obsessed with the need to preserve the revolutionary spirit against the revolution's success. That concern led the Convention to make the measurement of time assure that humanity remember that its institutions are its own.

At the other pole from the Revolutionary calendar's announcement that time is history stands the passive acceptance of time as it is in the *Shepheardes Calander*. A classic of pastoral, Spenser's poem represents the works of the seasons and the months rather than of human agents. Whereas the Convention sought to compel assent to the validity of its own means of meaning, Spenser's shepherds inscribe themselves in a discourse already formed. The Revolutionary calendar invented new signs to state the creation of a new world; the *Shepheardes Calander*, like pastoral works in general, accepted as such a static system and the static world it represented.

At least from the days when Virgil chose to label his earthly paradise with the name of a most unidyllic region called Arcadia, another distinguishing feature of pastoral has been a resolutely antimimetic character. Theoreticians of the genre are unanimous in decrying efforts to insert description of the real activity of real shepherds into poetry whose subject has nothing to do with rural life.

> Au contraire, cet Autre, abject en son langage,
> Fait parler ses Bergers, comme on parle au village.
> Ses vers plats et grossiers, dépouillez d'agrément,
> Toujours baisent la terre, et rampent tristement.

> [P]astoral is an image of what they call the Golden Age. So we are not to describe our shepherds as shepherds at this day really are, but as they may be conceiv'd then to have been. . . . We must therefore use some illusion to render a pastoral delightful.

> It seems natural for a young poet to initiate himself by pastorals, which, not professing to imitate real life, require no experience.[9]

The purpose of pastoral language is thus to abolish the appearance of reference to the world. Meaning is achieved by overt, conscious, and consistent allusions to the always already said. Pastoral does not conceal but proclaims its intertextuality, making it in fact the characteristic by which it is identified and assessed. The *Shepheardes Calander* is about neither shepherds nor time. It is an exercise in a particular way of signifying whose literary ancestors are the ineluctable preconditions of its intelligibility.

Structural linguistics and poststructuralist philosophers have argued that, at some deep level, the semiotic destruction and creation of the French Revolution were also only exercises within the confines of a received system.

Regardless of whether we consider those arguments convincing, there is undeniably a level—one which literary criticism must address—in which iconoclastic utterances like the Revolutionary calendar are different from self-consciously conventional literature. In place of the pastoral's subtext, the corpus of all other pastorals, the language of the Convention claimed as its subtext the concerted labor of human beings engaged in purposeful and collective action. To decide that the present year shall be called "An I de la République" instead of 1792 is to refuse (however misguidedly) former ways of meaning. To write about shepherds in love in the spring is to accept (however brilliantly) inherited conceptions of what makes sense.

Pastoral discourse is language that does not pretend that its signifying matrix is anything except other words; historical discourse is language that directs attention to the circumstances that gave it meaning. The play with these two forms of speech in *Quatrevingt-Treize* is extraordinary in the extent to which it repeats the irreconcilability of the interpretive conventions each requires. The same terms convey contradictory messages as the novel switches between its two stylistic registers. Children, guillotines, flowers, armies, dawns, and slogans are not static entities whose sense is fixed, but vessels whose semantic content is determined by the vision of the world implicit in the discourse speaking their names. In the Envoy of the *Shepheardes Calander*, Colin Clout announces the eternal value of his poetry:

> Loe I have made a Calander for every yeare,
> That steele in strength and time in durance shall outweare;
> And if I marked well the starres revolution
> It shall continue till the worlds dissolution.

In contrast to this assurance of a way of marking time that is guaranteed universal permanence, the Convention chose to name time by signs whose currency was contingent on the sociopolitical form assumed by a single speech community. This general distinction between history and eternity is reflected in that between the cyclical meaning of *revolution* in Spenser's "starres revolution" and the awesomely linear meaning of the French cognate in the Convention's words. The same word signifies the contradictory concepts of an assured return and an assured termination. To choose one or the other interpretation is to choose irreconcilable visions of humanity's place in time, and Hugo's text continually forces such choices as it displays its characters acting out a narrative structured by analogous elimination of possible ways to understand.

In playing on the mutually exclusive visions of historical and pastoral discourse, *Quatrevingt-Treize* incorporates a dichotomy which has often grounded alternative social philosophies. When the weight of history, of time as human action, seems too great to bear, people often translate their desire to escape into an obsession with cyclical phenomena. Paul Fussell catalogued the British people's "Arcadian recourses" in World War I,[10] and many authors who wrote of World War II highlighted the clash between its horrors and pastoral visions of rural occupations in a natural world. Tadeusz Borowski's remarkable stories of concentration camp life contain striking examples: "The vision from the window is almost pastoral—not one cremo in sight."[11] "Where Auschwitz stands today, three years ago there were villages and farms. There were rich meadows, shaded country lanes, apple orchards."[12] When Borowski combines the camp slang *cremo* with the concept of a *pastoral vision* or contrasts the meaning which history gave to Auschwitz with that which popular verse gives shaded country lanes, he creates the same dissonance established by devices like the alternating languages of the sun and the guillotine in *Quatrevingt-Treize*. Like Borowski, Hugo juxtaposes gratingly dissonant *écritures*.

In their discussions of nineteenth-century ideologues' tendency to naturalize the form of the bourgeois state, Marxist thinkers like the Lukács of *History and Class Consciousness* have furnished further evidence that nature and history are the armatures of contradictory visions of the world. After the success of the bourgeois revolution against aristocratic political structures, the revolution's beneficiaries began to conceive of history as a completed process. Guizot's notorious "The class struggle is over" was the overt statement of a social conception more frequently appearing as a tendency to represent transitory institutions as eternal phenomena no more subject to human intervention than the sequence of summer and winter. The fear of what can happen if society is historical often underlies an unconscious desire to conceive of society and its acts as natural. Those who made the French Revolution did not share that fear. The Convention's abolition of old signs whose human origin had been forgotten constrained recognition that human deeds in time have created society and that human deeds in time can blow it apart. The same recognition is implicit in historical discourse in *Quatrevingt-Treize*.

For Claude Lévi-Strauss, the dichotomy between historical and natural time has implications which are not limited to the modern West. *The Savage Mind* distinguishes between "cold" and "hot" societies,

> the former seeking, by the institutions they give themselves, to annul the possible effects of historical factors on their equilibrium and continuity in a quasi-automatic fashion; the latter resolutely internalizing the historical process and making it the moving power of its development. . . . Some [historical sequences] while existing in duration, are of a recurrent nature; the annual cycle of the seasons, for instance, or that of individual life or that of exchanges of goods and services within the social group. These sequences raise no problem because they are periodically repeated in duration without their structure necessarily undergoing any change. . . . [The procedure cold societies use to confront nonrecurrent events] consists not in denying the historical process but in admitting it as a form without content. There is indeed a before and an after, but their sole significance lies in reflecting each other.[13]

That passage is pertinent to Hugo's novel for several reasons. First, it succinctly identifies the common ground of the text's two major instances of recurrent phenomena, natural cycles and life cycles, in its reference to the fact that cold societies readily incorporate the temporal sequences of the seasons and of individual growth. Moreover, Lévi-Strauss aptly defines the epistemological function which the discourse of cycles assumes in *Quatrevingt-Treize*: validation of a world in which history is a form without content, in which before and after have significance only because they reflect one another. Gauvain, Lantenac, and Cimourdain seem to be caught up in a historical progression so powerfully linear that it instructed the world on what the meaning of history was; they are finally revealed to be caught up in the adult-child relationships whose stability also radiates from the tale of the Fléchard family. The novel's conclusion reflects a beginning that predated both its opening words and the historical event it ostensibly chose as its subject.

The epistemological effect of concentration on natural phenomena, which denies the significance of history, is perfectly congruent with the antimimetic character of pastoral language, which refers only to the world of words. Because the words of the French Revolution signify within *Quatrevingt-Treize*, the world of material things is also relevant to its message. When Cimourdain tells Gauvain that Robespierre, Marat, Danton, and Saint-Just have become names that are worth armies (p. 287), he is describing the interchange between signification and history on which the novel never ceases to play.

In introducing the castle that will come to symbolize the feudal order, *Quatrevingt-Treize* takes pains to specify that the words which describe a castle do not mean to us what they meant to our ancestors.

> C'est là ce que nos aïeux appelaient un "cul de basse-fosse." La chose ayant disparu, le nom pour nous n'a plus de sens. Grâce à la révolution, nous entendons prononcer ces mots-là avec indifférence. (p. 298)

Passages like that one make explicit the equivalency between semiotic force and society's historical development which underlies all of the historical discourse in *Quatrevingt-Treize*. Pastoral discourse displays in contrast forms recurring as predictably as the events of pastoral time.

Ultimately, as we have seen, *Quatrevingt-Treize* seeks to validate pastoral over historical representation. History is an absolute reality, and the language of history has absolute value. But there is also a contradictory reality, which requires for its expression signs more permanent than those that pass with human institutions. The text arranges its truths hierarchically, as is most obvious in the spatial metaphors—"above royalty, above revolutions," and so forth—which punctuate Gauvain's decision to release Lantenac.

"Gauvain, républicain, croyait être, et était, dans l'absolu. Un absolu supérieur venait de se révéler. Au-dessus de l'absolu révolutionnaire, il y a l'absolu humain" (p. 431). The *absolu supérieur*, the *lumière supérieure* (p. 438), and the *vérité supérieure* (p. 442) are uniformly ahistorical. But they do not, they cannot extinguish the hard light of historical action and of language adequate to *its* truth.

Hugo's expressed intention in writing *Quatrevingt-Treize* was to defuse the historical signs exemplified by his title.

> [J]e veux dégager la révolution de l'horreur dont on a cru lui faire une force; dans ce livre, je la fais dominer par l'innocence; je tâche de jeter sur ce chiffre effrayant, *93*, un rayon apaisant. Je veux que le progrès continue de faire loi, et cesse de faire peur.[14]

In one sense, *Quatrevingt-Treize* accomplishes this purpose. The novel is in fact dominated by innocence; it does radiate the calming light of an ever-returning sun. In another sense, however, the novel fails miserably to realize its author's intentions. The peaceful light is cast not on the revolution but on a representation of the world which cannot communicate revolutions. It illuminates not history but recurrences. Although the text includes a form of discourse in which 93 is only a number between 92 and 94, it also demonstrates that this discourse cannot encode the homophonous name of the year of the Terror. The text sanitizes *quatre-vingt-treize* while proclaiming that *Quatrevingt-Treize* and *An II de la République* derive their meaning from humanity's capacity to seize the divine right to name and define.

Let us look again at the Hugolian intertext of *quatrevingt-treize*.

> Dans l'histoire où tu luis comme en une fournaise,
> Reste seul à jamais, Titan quatrevingt-treize!
> Rien d'aussi grand que toi ne viendrait après toi.

> Quiconque sondera ce puits: Quatrevingt-treize,
> Sentira se cabrer et s'enfuir son esprit.[15]

Quatrevingt-Treize of course conveys meaning because it is a nodal point on a structure which the mind has no difficulty assimilating. But the mind "rears up and gallops away" because the sign "glows in history" as well as signifying through semiosis. *Quatrevingt-Treize* confronts historical meaning that refuses enclosure in the universe of discourse with intertextually well behaved language that makes such enclosure its reason for being. The peaceful absolute of language which signifies as language should is set beside language whose meaning constrains recognition of another absolute—chaotic, disturbing, and historical.

4

Il y a des mots qui font vivre

When Gabriel Péri was shot by the Nazis, Paul Eluard wrote the extraordinarily moving poem which contains the line quoted in this chapter's title, "there are words that give life." Eluard's examples of those words include both the vehicles of abstract semantic features—*freedom, warmth, comrade*—and the referential signs of autobiographical experience, the (proper) names of villages and friends. A comparable refusal to separate semantics and experience, nodal points and referential labels, typifies the rhetoric of the French Revolution, which consistently attached signification as well as significance to events.

For Eluard, the corpus of life-giving words is open-ended, and Péri's death "added" to the list. There are lives that give meaning as surely as there are words that give life. The French Revolution analogously viewed the signifying process as an act rather than an abstraction. To accept or reject the signs by which the Revolution named itself was to accept or reject the definition's implementation in the world. *Quatrevingt-Treize* consistently plays on the revolutionary lexicon's ability to evoke the events which made words give life, another reason why criticism of the novel must combine historical inquiry with formal linguistic analysis.

The general contradiction between the two stylistic registers in Hugo's novel is reflected in individual oppositions between passages evoking history's capacity to change meaning and passages presenting language and existence as equally static. In order to examine these microcosmic instances of the novel's dialectic, it is necessary to choose a section for detailed discussion. The one that immediately suggests itself is the novel's opening chapter, which not only sets in motion the principal narrative sequence but also displays features of a self-contained prologue. The Parisian troops' discovery of the Fléchard family occurs long before the family is integrated into the stories of Gauvain, Cimourdain, and Lantenac, a separation highlighted by the fact that the *forest* setting for the discovery opens a book entitled "En *Mer*." Furthermore, the first chapter of *Quatrevingt-Treize* summarizes its entire thematic argument. The novel is organized around progressive transcendence of characters' political understanding of the purely human Fléchards. The prologue prefigures that general move in its description of Parisian soldiers as they first interpret the family by the historical hermeneutic identifying Breton peasants as enemies and then recognize the gross inapplicability of their original interpretation. As it will later show its protagonists doing, *Quatrevingt-Treize* opens by depicting minor characters who learn to respond to human misery instead of historical imperatives. The prologue's developing verbal structure constitutes a lexical correlative to this moral lesson.

1. What we have here is a failure to communicate.

And a stupefyingly complete one. When the Parisians discover the peasant family, their attempt at a political interview elicits no political information whatever. Misunderstandings, blank stares, and *je ne sais pas* prove the mother's total inability to decode the words she hears.

> —Je te demande quelles sont tes opinions politiques?
> —Je ne sais pas ça. . . .
> —Arrive au fait. Qui es-tu?
> —Je ne sais pas.
> —Tu ne sais pas qui tu es?
> —Nous sommes des gens qui nous sauvons.
> —De quel parti es-tu?
> —Je ne sais pas.
> —Es-tu des bleus? Es-tu des blancs? Avec qui es-tu?
> —Je suis avec mes enfants. . . .
> —Comment, tu ne sais pas qui a tué ton mari?
> —Non.
> —Est-ce un bleu? Est-ce un blanc?
> —C'est un coup de fusil. (pp. 12-18)

Immediately striking in this *dialogue de sourds* is the scorn for verisimilitude it displays. The possibility of anyone actually emitting Michelle's responses seems to be of no concern beside the need to establish a linguistic and epistemological gulf between her and the Republicans. Such a primacy of thematic concerns over mimetic constraints generally characterizes Hugo's fictions, in which blatant disregard for novelistic convention often serves, as here, to emphasize the points being made at the expense of realism. In the preceding excerpts and elsewhere in the introductory dialogue, the question to be asked is not whether a remark could have been made but how its (improbable) occurrence contributes to the text's global self-definition.

The first line between Michelle and her interlocutors is in the nature of the vocabulary which elicits her protestations of incomprehension. Words like *parti* or *opinions politiques* belong to a corpus apparently unknown to the apolitical mother, who reacts to them only by refusing to respond to them. More important than this noninterpretation are the mother's misinterpretations, which demonstrate that she and the revolutionaries are exercising mutually incompatible decoding procedures. In linguistic parlance, "selection restriction" denotes the process by which participants in the communicative circuit select the appropriate meaning of ambivalent words. Assessment of the form of discourse in which a polysemic construction appears restricts the meaning we can assign it. For example, our understanding of *Let's go to the bank* will vary according to whether it follows *I need some money* or *I'm tired of rowing*. Since we assume discourse coherence, the various signifieds of *bank* do not impede our ability to choose the one suited to the context. Communicative breakdowns occur when speakers differ in their assessments of the form of discourse they are employing.

Just such differing assessments are what make interrogation of Michelle Fléchard a communicative disaster. The soldiers perceive meaning as political and speak accordingly. The mother is monolingually restricted to a code in which political significance is inexpressible. Although *avec*, for instance, is subject to a variety of selection restrictions, its meaning in a political context is clear. When the sergeant asks the peasant whom she is with, he is straight-forwardly requesting a statement of ideological sympathy. But his sense does not exist for the mother, who understands *avec* not as *politically adherent to* but as *physically and emotionally bound to*. She consequently responds with a stunning non sequitur, the statement that she is "with her children." Similarly, "Qui es-tu?" is in context a demand for political identity, which for Michelle is no identity at all. As she understands the cause of her husband's death to be a rifle shot instead of historical conflict, so she represents herself not as a member of a party but as a human running away. The sergeant's imperious "Arrive au fait" is particularly ironic, for Michelle's language allows her neither to express nor to understand what the Parisians consider a "fait."

Quatrevingt-Treize thus begins with a dramatic (in both senses) illustration of the fact that historical and pastoral discourse impose contradictory ways of representing and understanding. The peasant lives in a world of natural time and family ties, the soldiers in history and engagement. That difference appears in the text as verbal forms which do not survive translation from one world to the other. Two dominant characteristics distinguish the Revolution's language. First, words have a temporally specific sense; second, historical action is the origin and preserver of that sense. Neither characteristic applies to the mother's language, where children are children as surely as the summer remains the summer, the lily and the star remain the lily and the star.

The binary opposition *bleu/blanc*, whose recurrence in the sergeant's questions elicits nothing from Michelle Fléchard, manifests both features of historical language. The first member of the pair conveys a meaning that neither existed before the Revolution nor survived after it. Although some later periods of French history assigned political content to *bleu*, it was subsequently opposed to *rouge* as well as to *blanc* and thus designated a moderate rather than a radical stance. The equation of *bleu* and *blanc* with *revolutionary* and *reactionary* was a lexical fact limited to Auerbach's "perfectly definite historical moment," one whose referential specificity is further enhanced by the fact that the Vendée rebellion first gave *bleu* its political meaning.

Quatrevingt-Treize will continually contrast the historically precise opposition between *bleu* and *blanc* to the transhistorical signification of pastoral words. As we have seen, the sentence, "L'oncle commande les blancs, le neveu commande les bleus" (p. 246), appears in a passage whose development demonstrates the superiority of the temporally grounded antagonism between Blue and White to the immemorial bond between uncle and nephew. The 1793 meaning of Blue and White can dominate even more intimate familial ties: "le père sert dans les blancs, le fils sert dans les bleus. Rencontre. Bataille. Le père fait prisonnier son fils, et lui brûle la cervelle" (p. 32). When Michelle Fléchard, who is with her children, refuses to respond to the demand for a Blue/White choice, her implicit denunciation of historical meaninglessness also affirms kinship terms as radiantly meaningful.

Bleu also displays the second characteristic of a historical lexicon, the assertion that those who seize the right to make the world also earn the right to make its meaning. Originally a contemptuous name imposed on Republicans by the Vendée rebels, whose color was of course white, *bleu* was condemnatory as well as denotative. The Royalists' scorn for their opponents produced bad puns like this: "It's blue pottery, it can't take fire."[1] When the Republican successes made *bleu* a label to be proudly claimed (and gave rise to another saying, "blue clothes frayed by victories"),[2] the word had undergone the same historical transformation as "sans-culottes." Both terms were opprobrious until collective action in specific conditions transformed them into encomia.

That action also transformed the sense of *patrie*, for the mother not a unit of language but undifferentiated noise.

>   –Quelle est ta patrie?
>   –Je ne sais pas, dit-elle.
>   –Comment, tu ne sais pas quel est ton pays?
>   –Ah! mon pays! Si fait.... c'est la métairie de Siscoignard, dans la paroisse d'Azé.
>   Ce fut le tour du sergent d'être stupéfait....
>   –Ce n'est pas une patrie, ça.
>   –C'est mon pays. (p. 12)

What makes *pays* and *patrie* so disparate that use of one dumbfounds speakers who use the other? Both words designate geographical situation, but as its etymology suggests, *patrie* expresses in addition the concept of a parent-child relationship between an area and its inhabitants, a filial bond to a political entity which Michelle Fléchard, the natural mother, cannot understand. In the schemata of formal semantics, *pays* and *patrie* would have congruent signifieds up to the point where the latter adds a feature of allegiance not found in the former. Although that additional feature is of course stored in the mental dictionary, the communicative breakdown it causes here evokes information included in mental encyclopedias. The sergeant is using a word that suggests human agents can create something resembling a parent.

The opposition between revolutionary creation of a fatherland and reactionary devotion to society as inherited was at the heart of the conflict between Paris and the provinces in 1793. *Quatrevingt-Treize* can therefore present the lexical pair which encapsulates this ideological distinction as a "summary" of the rebellion in the West: "*Pays, Patrie,* ces deux mots résument toute la guerre de Vendée" (p. 240). The words by which peasant and patriots fail to communicate in the prologue introduce an exemplary instance of the identity between verbal forms and historical themes in *Quatrevingt-Treize*.

Given Hugo's unique verbal sensitivity, it is not surprising that the *pays/patrie* opposition invokes a long tradition. From its introduction into French during the Renaissance, *patrie* competed for the semantic space already occupied by *pays*. Du Bellay, for instance, was rebuked in these terms for using yet another Latinate neologism: "Whoever has *pays* doesn't need *patrie*. . . . Recently the name *patrie* came obliquely into French with other Italian corruptions."[3] Although *patrie*, like other oblique Italian corruptions, flourished in its new language, it was slow to acquire its present meaning. In the entry for *patrie* in his *Dictionnaire philosophique*, for example, Voltaire made the word a near synonym for "comfortable place," in the process severing it from the idea of birthplace communicated in the same article by *pays*. The capacity of the semantic contrast between *pays* and *patrie* to summarize the Vendée rebellion, the sense of *patrie* to which Michelle Fléchard is deaf, was a specific creation of the Revolution.

And of the Revolution's most heroic period, which made *patrie* the emblem of struggle for definitive liberation from the old world. On July 11, 1792, revolutionary Paris began to define itself against the universe by declaring *la patrie en danger* and issuing a call for armed defense of the new society. Two weeks later, a band of southern *fédérés* responded by marching into Paris singing their own call to the fatherland's defense, a song to be known as the *Marseillaise* which began with a stirring appeal to the *enfants de la patrie*. Ten days after arriving in Paris, those same *fédérés* participated in the momentous events of August 10, 1792, when insurgents stormed the Tuileries, massacred the royal family's Swiss guard, and effectively destroyed a millenium of French monarchy.

As Albert Soboul and other historians have argued, August 10 was the day on which the Revolution actually became a national and social movement, a collective effort by citizens from all over France to transform the nature of their government. Those who performed that world-historical action immediately explained themselves by declaring that their violence against the king was necessary to "prevent the ruin of the *patrie*."[4] From that declaration to the Thermidorian reaction, *patrie* displayed the mystic character of a sign able to crystallize the purpose directing the titanic struggle of a people in revolutionary process. In a speech to the Convention in 1792, for instance, Saint-Just took a step toward recognition that the parent-child relationship between fatherland and citizens imposes paternal responsibility as well as filial loyalty. A people without the means of subsistence "has no *patrie*." Its leaders must "give it a *patrie*"[5] by guaranteeing the material prerequisites of human decency. Such utterances are possible only when the additional semantic feature which distinguishes *patrie* from *pays* is perceived as a linguistic fact whose communicative force is inseparable from historical action.

Roland went further. In his letter of resignation from the king's cabinet, he extracted *patrie* from the category of linguistic facts altogether, making it less a sign than a human creation present in the material world. "*Patrie* is not a word which imagination has been pleased to embellish; it is a being to which we have made sacrifices . . . which we have created by great efforts."[6] Frequently interrupted by "the most spirited applause" when read to the Assembly, the letter containing that quotation was printed and distributed to the eighty-three departments. It is legitimate to assume that its semiotic tenets, its announcement that the words of revolution are part and parcel of the deeds of revolution, was one of the reasons for its appeal. Those who were destroying an old world and building a new one required a lexicon able to keep pace.

For the lyrical author of the *Dictionnaire national et anecdotique*, the Revolution found *patrie* a void signifier and filled it with the most majestic of signifieds. "What a word yesterday, and what a word today! . . . the word *patrie* was formerly nothing but an empty sound because there is no *patrie* where there are bastilles, because there is no *patrie* where there are priests and hereditary judges or legislators, finally because there is no *patrie* where there is no *patrie*."[7] The concluding clause, tautological only in appearance, in fact asserts the identity between signification and history which was at the heart of the French Revolution's semiotic consciousness. Even when they leave signifiers unchanged, the events that alter men's lives also transform beyond recognition the symbolic forms that explain lives' meanings. "What a word yesterday, and what a word today!"

Revolutionary uses of *patrie* are directly related to the communicative breakdown in the prologue of *Quatrevingt-Treize*. For the Parisian soldiers living the Revolution, the supplementary seme of *patrie* depends not on semantic organization but on collective will. The declaration of *la patrie en danger* was a call to arms, the Marseilles volunteers gave substance to their status as children of the *patrie* by seizing the royal palace, Saint-Just saw *patrie* as a meaning to be achieved, Roland as a being which great efforts had created. Verbal meaning is the effect of the deeds that sustain it, which necessarily implies that the end of the deeds is the end of the meaning. It is this mutability, this concept of a connection between the variable events of history and the

apparently stable categories of language, that best defines the historical speech
alien to Michelle Fléchard. The peasant is with her children, a rifle shot killed
her husband, she is running away, her home is Azé parish—the words by which
she defines herself do not alter with human events. For one side of the introductory nondialogue, meaning is fixed and *natural*. For the other, it is a
newly created *social* fact.

The mother's encounter with revolutionary signification induces fear and
trembling as well as blank incomprehension.

> La mère était muette d'effroi.
> Le sergent lui cria:
> —N'ayez pas peur, nous sommes le bataillon du Bonnet-Rouge.
> La femme trembla de la tête aux pieds. . . .
> —Le bataillon de la ci-devant Crois-Rouge, ajouta la vivandière. (p. 10)

Confronting a woman terrified by the unknown, the sergeant reasonably
assumes that identifying himself and his comrades will calm her. His effect
is the opposite of what he intended, a textual fact which again points outward,
to the historical locus of the identifying words. Along with the pike, the red
cap was the quintessential symbol of militant Parisian revolutionaries. And,
like the pike, it was indissolubly associated with cataclysmic events. The red
cap's popularity directly reflected the Revolution's development from bourgeois
moderation to sans-culotte militancy and back again. It was after invasion of
the Tuileries on August 10 that it became almost universal. In sharp decline
during the Thermidorian reaction, use of the red cap disappeared after the
Prairial repression destroyed the remnants of the Revolution's militant period.[8]

Michelle Fléchard thus trembles on perceiving sounds which mark as well as
signify, which are a synecdoche of historical signification in general. As if
sensing this cause for her fear, the vivandière begins to display the compassion
which will characterize her throughout the political interview and reverts to an
old sign system, that which named her section *Croix-Rouge* instead of *Bonnet-
Rouge*. But she also uses a marker of history, the phrase *ci-devant*, which was
the Revolution's most consistent and ominous assertion that past semiotics,
old ways of segmenting the universe, were no longer valid. Forced to decode a
representation in which history is essential rather than accidental, the mother
sinks into quivering stupefaction.

The progressive popularization and rejection of the red cap itself is mirrored
in the fortunes of its name. The battalion's designation is that of the Parisian
section from which its soldiers came, a section which in fact changed its name
from Croix-Rouge to Bonnet-Rouge in 1793. The move to rebaptize Paris's
sections received a memorable statement of purpose when the leaders of the
Beaubourg section, recognizing that the more "the *patrie* is in danger, the more
citizens must unite," decided to adopt the name of Réunion because, in their

prophetically ambivalent judgement, "Beaubourg" was *insignifiant*—insignificant and nonsignifying.[9]

Like many other section names, the successive rebaptisms of what was originally the Croix-Rouge section demonstrate a will to give the world labels adequate to its newly created meaning. The name was first changed not because Croix-Rouge was nonsignifying but because it signified the wrong thing. The section rejected the cross because it no longer wished "to bear a name that could perpetuate fanaticism."[10] The new name was an eloquent statement of revolutionary commitment; as a consequence, it endured only as long as that commitment itself. In Germinal, Year III, sans-culotte resistance to the Thermidorian reaction was severely repressed. Simultaneously, the Bonnet-Rouge section became the Bonnet-de-la-Liberté section.

This second change is particularly interesting for our purposes because it suggests the extent to which verbal forms embody political stances. *Bonnet rouge* and *bonnet de la liberté* had the same referent, a Phrygian cap. But the words *bonnet rouge* were too inflammatory to be admitted. A lexical change gelded the iconographic object, whose original name was later to appear most commonly in the Restoration cliché *hideux bonnet rouge*. The Grand Larousse of 1865 speaks of the "repulsion" which *bonnet rouge* had been arousing for half a century, an unintended tribute to the success of the revolutionary sections' efforts to free themselves from "nonsignifying" words. The names they chose, and the deeds by which they defined them, came to signify most forcefully indeed.

Even the neutralized *bonnet de la liberté* was too highly charged to survive, however. The Prairial repression that effectively ended the Revolution as a popular movement also saw the Bonnet-de-la-Liberté section rebaptized with the resolutely ahistorical name of *Ouest*. At exactly the same time, the pike, that other great symbol of sans-culotte fury, also disappeared from the map of Paris when the Piques section became the Place-Vendôme section. The Revolution was over. Its signs, synecdoches of historical signifying systems, were accordingly replaced by those expressing the geographical constants of a pastoral universe.

As the frontispiece of his *Mémorial des siècles* volume on the French Revolution, Gérard Walter reproduces a drawing from a pamphlet published during the Terror and bearing the characteristically flamboyant title *Report to the sans-culottes of the French Republic by the very high, very powerful and very prompt Lady Guillotine*. The top half of the drawing shows an arm emerging from clouds, its hand holding a blue sword. Arm and sword together form an elongated "V" which frames an eye, itself enclosed in a sun radiating yellow lines to all points. From the hand is suspended a scale of justice, and on the scale is squarely set a red cap.

The lower half of the picture, less symbolic and more grisly, depicts a half-dozen bodies and a half-dozen heads which have been separated from them. Both bodies and heads wear the royal and ecclesiastical insignia of the Revolution's enemies. In the lower right corner, baskets display an assortment of other heads. The picture, crudely drawn throughout, is particularly crude in the lower half, further contrasted to the brightly colored symbols above by being in grey and white. An inscription at the base states that the "Law is a sword which must without distinction cut down all that rises above it."

The two halves of this picture are intriguing in their use of two forms of semiosis. The iconography of the upper half can be adequately decoded without reference to the Revolution. Justice's sword and scale, like the all-seeing eye of the sun, are classical symbols whose origin is lost in legend. Even the red cap, as the 1865 Grand Larousse is at pains to specify, has, as antiquity's sign for freed slaves, long symbolized liberty. Justice, vigilance, and freedom thus appear as traditional symbolic forms in a harmonious composition neatly divided by a broken line and vividly colored in the primaries red, yellow, and blue.

But this classical harmony and symbolism—this orthodox signification—is only half of the picture. The other half, with its gory severed heads and mutilated bodies, both destroys compositional harmony and creates historically specific meaning. As a totality, the picture defines the scale as that of revolutionary justice, identifies the sword with the guillotine, assimilates the all-seeing eye to vigilance committees, and, most emphatically, makes the red cap symbolize not a freed slave but a militant sans-culotte. The vigilance, justice, and freedom at issue are not Platonic ideas, the timeless signs of timeless abstractions, but the specific categories of a particular moment. Accordingly, a memorable representation of the violence that created the moment, that gave symbols a historically specific sense, underlies the symbols themselves. The picture is a whole whose parts cannot be isolated.

Yet that is precisely what someone, presumably the *Mémorial des siècles* editor, attempted. Although Walter's frontispiece reproduces the entire picture, only the upper half appears on the cover. Like the nineteenth century's *hideux bonnet rouge*, this 1967 excision is unconscious tribute to the abiding capacity of the Revolution's semiotics to convey the disturbing possibility of the Revolution's recurrence.

The picture accompanying Lady Guillotine's report exemplifies the necessity of recognizing the extratextual function of words like *patrie* and *bonnet rouge* in order to understand their value in Hugo's novel. As the symbols in the upper half of the picture can be considered in isolation, so the lexicon of historical discourse in *Quatrevingt-Treize* can be discussed apart from historical events. The featural congruence and contrast between *pays* and *patrie* and the *croix rouge* → *bonnet rouge* transformation of course have purely formal value. But, like the decision to reproduce only part of the picture from the Terror on Walter's cover, discussion of that value alone would mutilate the signification which 1793 and Hugo's novelistic representation of it actually validated. Like the pictorial combination of justice's symbols and the guillotine's victims, *Quatrevingt-Treize* does not abstract the signs of revolution from the events which made them signs.

The primary feature of the prologue is perfectly straightforward: peasant and patriots employ mutually incomprehensible forms of discourse. However, underlying that textual fact are disparate conceptions of what can and should be signified. The cross-purposes conversation that opens *Quatrevingt-Treize* is structured around the distinction between a lexicon with historically specific value and a lexicon transcending all social changes, between a subtext of political cataclysm and a subtext of other words. The peasant mother hears something new when she can understand only what is old.

Historical discourse in *Quatrevingt-Treize* is of course not to be confused with textual reproduction of actual utterances. The novel assimilates historical signs and adapts them to its purposes, as is most apparent in factual errors. For instance, the Croix-Rouge section did not change its name to Bonnet-Rouge until October 1793. Since the events of the prologue ostensibly take place in May of 1793, the historical sign which made Michelle Fléchard tremble is actually anachronistic. For another example, consider communicative breakdowns like this: " 'Quel âge a ce môme?' demanda-t-elle. La mère ne comprit pas" (p. 11). *Môme* is Parisian argot, one of the words strongly associated with the capital which Hugo continually put in the mouth of Gavroche. The chapter of *Les Misérables* entitled "Gavroche tire parti de Napoléon ie Grand," for instance, contains what amounts to a morphological exercise on *môme* and its derivatives. The fact that *môme* did not enter French until after the Revolution and Empire is immaterial to its textual function as another marker of speech that is historically (and not chronologically) determinate, in this case as a sign of the city which sustained the Revolution. Although historical discourse in *Quatrevingt-Treize* insistently evokes precise situations of utterance, the text never attempts the impossible task of reproducing them.

Why does *Quatrevingt-Treize* set its first chapter apart from the body of the novel it introduces and organize the chapter so foregrounded around a tedious series of misunderstandings? Because of its need to supply from the beginning a hermeneutic clue to the codes it will confront and contrast, a need all the more imperious because those codes demand normally incompatible interpretive operations. The text's sequences of historical and pastoral language require that its words be considered alternately as vehicles of "literary" content and as indicators of a historical reality refusing structuration. The prologue of *Quatrevingt-Treize* constitutes a metalingual commentary on the novel as a whole.

In his seminal essay on "Linguistics and Poetics,"[11] Roman Jakobson defines the metalingual function of language as that which directs attention to the codes being used. His examples are exactly the sort of misunderstanding repeated in Hugo's prologue. When messages do not communicate, the explanation is to be sought in the nature of the code in which they are emitted, in the mistaken assessments of discourse forms that produce inappropriate selection restrictions. The opening of *Quatrevingt-Treize* stridently demonstrates that a mother's code is not a revolution's. The latter, developing new signs to name new realities, presents signification as the effect of actions taken to produce and preserve it. In direct contrast, pastoral discourse uses old signs to express old truths and derives its communicative force from a network of words equally insulated from their referents. The metalingual commentary which begins *Quatrevingt-Treize* embodies the irresolvable otherness of the forms of writing the text will incorporate. As a guillotine to flowering heather, so is the language of 1793 to a widow with children.

2. *Ou on en a eu*

The very first words of *Quatrevingt-Treize*, "Dans les derniers jours de mai, 1793," begin to show how the novel will develop a signifying whole so as to orient interpretation of its parts. Those words evoke distinct complexes of associations. Whereas "last days of May" is a stock sequence in the language of pastoral exultation in merry months and joyous certainties, "1793" names the year in which Western society became aware of itself as a historical entity. In isolation, either component of the novel's opening, the month or the year, could be taken to subsume the implications of the other.

If the historical year in fact dominates the springtime month, it is because the language which follows is insistently referential. The previously discussed accumulation of historical allusions in the novel's first sentence is followed by further heaping of referential terms: battles, proper names, dates, and toponyms. One of the last, that of the Bon-Conseil section, is especially suggestive of the connection between the words in the text and the circumstances they designate. In 1792, the Mauconseil (Bad Advice) section changed its name to Bon-Conseil (Good Advice). The textual appearance of the newly chosen name has the dual purpose of augmenting an already copious historical vocabulary and suggesting the connection between revolutionary words and revolutionary practice. "Bon-Conseil" appears because that was the section on whose "advice" troops were sent to the Vendée (p. 6). This novel about the war in the West begins with an allusion to the war's origin in an area whose name recalls the age's will toward a language which was less a closed system than an open form for expressing the new.

Hugo's introductory lines further reject pastoral interpretation by making spring months the setting for human action rather than proof that nature's rebirth eternally occurs. On April 25, Paris decided to send troops to the Vendée; on April 28, the Commune ordered no quarter for the rebels; on May 1, 12,000 volunteers left for the West; by the end of May, 8,000 of them were dead. Such constructions, by inserting the springtime months into a linear progression incompatible with pastoral's cyclical vision, contribute to establishing an interpretive stance that precludes assigning its normal value to the Romantic language of springtime joys. When such language occurs, no matter how great the harmony of its internal organization, it is a dissonant intrusion in a previously defined whole.

> Tout était plein de fleurs; on avait autour de soi une tremblante muraille de branches d'où tombait la charmante fraîcheur des feuilles; des rayons de soleil trouaient çà et là les ténèbres vertes; à terre, le glaïeul, la flambe des marais, le narcisse des prés, la gênotte, cette petite fleur qui annonce le beau temps, le safran printanier, brodaient et passementaient un profond tapis de végétation où fourmillaient toutes les formes de la mousse, depuis celle qui ressemble à la chenille jusqu'à celle qui ressemble à l'étoile. (p. 7)

This long sentence, no part of which is remotely capable of historical reference, also abounds in the marks of bucolic May writing. Saccharine phrasing, profuse floral nomenclature that generates *gênotte* by fabricating signs from signs, verb tenses limited to vague imperfects and eternal presents—all evoke generic conventions directly opposed to historical narrative. For Paul Fussell, "the opposite of experiencing moments of war is proposing moments of pastoral."[12] Just that proposal is made by the nature sentence interpolated in the referential language which begins *Quatrevingt-Treize*. As if the connotative hierarchy previously established for "last days of May" and "1793" had been overturned, the text suddenly appears to invoke a different interpretive approach.

The appearance is a fleeting one, however, so much so that its presence only affirms the dominance of historical meaning. Because the language of floral weavers and starry moss occurs within a presentation of political turbulence, the reader is invited to imitate the hermeneutic processes adopted by the Republican soldiers, whose assessment of the world in which they live causes them to interpret the marks of Arcadia as signs of Armageddon.

> Le bois semblait désert. Le bataillon redoublait de prudence. Solitude, donc défiance. On ne voyait personne; raison de plus pour redouter quelqu'un. (p. 8)

Those sentences constitute a triple oxymoronic progression—*bois désert* → *prudence, solitude* → *défiance, personne* → *quelqu'un*—whose middle term assumes the graphic form of a simple exercise in logical consequence: "Solitude, donc défiance." It would be difficult to devise a more succinct and lucid illustration of the peculiar interpretive attitude the text is eliciting. Because they recognize a historically molded whole, the soldiers assign historical significance to all of its parts. The global configuration of the words which present their suspicion duplicates its effect. The hackneyed signifiers of pastoral writing acquire signifieds incompatible with their normal message. Hymns to flowers that bloom in the spring propose a moment of pastoral, but the dominant language of historical conflict grounds the text in an age of war.

The beginning of *Quatrevingt-Treize* consequently seems to preestablish a hierarchical relationship between the codes employed by Michelle Fléchard and her Republican interrogators. Introductory validation of historical understanding denigrates the mother's inability to respond to the words conveying it. This implicit semiotic judgement is perfectly harmonious with the prologue's seeming thematic concerns; the novel does after all open by depicting heralds of the future freeing victims of the past. The Republican language which Michelle hears for the first time informs her of exhilarating concepts like a *patrie* and liberating events like the rebaptism of a *ci-devant* king as Louis Capet. The Parisians' material beneficence affirms the worth of their ideological mission. Giving food to the hungry and shelter to the homeless, they take widow and orphans under their protection as enthusiastically as they speak of the Revolution. Verbal, ideological, and material components all coalesce in the two words that conclude the prologue, *Venez, citoyenne.* As the miserable, starving, ragged family leaves the wilderness of the Old Regime with unexpected prospects for a fully human life, another radiant new word filled with the hope of the future enters the text. The revolutionary passion for equality and fraternity was clearly manifest when all deference to rank was abolished and replaced by the universal titles *citoyen* and *citoyenne*, whose use in the thousand encounters of daily life concretized the ideals whose abstract formulation gave rise to the most famous of the Revolution's slogans.

The communicative barrier between Michelle Fléchard and the Revolution's missionaries thus seems to derive from the former's crushing oppression. "Parlant une langue morte, ce qui est faire habiter une tombe à sa pensée" (p. 221), the peasant encounters language adequate to the vibrant thought that human possibilities are limitless. Nowhere are her verbal and social backwardness more apparent than when Michelle narrates her family background.

> Mon père était infirme et ne pouvait travailler à cause qu'il avait reçu des coups de bâton que le seigneur, son seigneur, notre seigneur, lui avait fait donner, ce qui était une bonté, parce que mon père avait pris un lapin, pour le fait de quoi on était jugé à mort; mais le seigneur lui avait fait grâce et avait dit: Donnez-lui seulement cent coups de bâton. (p. 14)

Awkward phrasing (*à cause qu'il*), mindless recitation (*le seigneur, son seigneur, notre seigneur*) and unconscious irony (*ce qui était une bonté*) express the effect of imprisonment in the old society. The peasant goes on to tell how, although her grandfather was imprisoned for his Protestantism and her father-in-law hanged by the king, her husband died fighting for king, church, and lord. This story of devotion to oppressors provokes an energetic protest from a Republican grenadier.

C'est que c'est tout de même un véritable massacrement pour l'entendement d'un honnête homme . . . que de voir des iroquois de la Chine qui ont eu leur beau-père estropié par le seigneur, leur grand-père galérien par le curé et leur père pendu par le roi, et qui se battent, nom d'un petit bonhomme! et qui se fichent en révolte et qui se font écrabouiller pour le seigneur, le curé et le roi! (p. 17)

One could quibble that this outburst would improve with less of Gavroche's colorful cuteness and more of Hébert's obscene rage. Nevertheless, the grenadier's speech furnishes a superb counterpoint to the halting phrases and stultified thought which provoked it. The content of the Republican's tirade is a powerful statement of why the Revolution was necessary, its style a forceful reminder that new forms of eloquence accompanied France's struggle for a new way of life. When those who had been denied the floor took it by force in Paris's clubs and sectional assemblies, their assaults on outmoded verbal forms were as violent as their rejection of outmoded social hierarchies. In his excellent notes to the Garnier edition of *Quatrevingt-Treize*, Jean Boudout chooses the grenadier's speech as the appropriate place to signal Hugo's desire, "manifest in this opening scene," to depict the Vendée rebellion as both wrong and wrong-headed. A summary of the prologue's metalingual commentary converges with the culmination of its ideological message, for the staggering contrast between revolutionary and peasant language confirms all previous suggestions of the former's superiority.

Or does it? There are problems with the assumption that the grenadier's speech exemplifies the text's preferred form of expression. First, it is clear that the potential beneficiary of the new vision does not even perceive the new code which transmits it; Michelle Fléchard is not listening. Moreover, the Republican sergeant declares the grenadier's outburst wholly inappropriate. After ordering silence, the officer says that such "eloquence" is out of place because "nous ne sommes pas ici au club de la section des Piques" (p. 17). The rhetoric of sectional clubs, developed to express the revolutionary vision, is declared unsuitable in the mouths of men at war to realize the revolutionary goals. Since the red cap and the pike were the major symbols of militant sans-culottes, the admonition to a sans-culotte from the Bonnet-Rouge section not to use the language of the Piques section symbolically declares the irrelevance of militancy itself. A memorable instance of the language of 1793 leads to proclamation that it is an unwanted and alien discourse.

The Republican who here asserts that silence is preferable to political eloquence had earlier been the subject of a narrative comment to the same effect. After his inability to make Michelle Fléchard understand *patrie*,

Le sergent, qui était un peu beau parleur, continua l'interrogatoire.
—On a des parents, que diable! ou on en a eu. Qui es-tu? Parle.
La femme écouta, ahurie, cet—*ou on en a eu*—qui ressemblait plus à un cri de bête qu'à une parole humaine. (p. 13)

If it is a metalingual statement that historically precise language is best suited to its subject, the first chapter of *Quatrevingt-Treize* uses very curious techniques. It is not the verbally backward victim of subjugation but the bearer of the Revolution's gospel who snorts *ou on en a eu*, its steadily rising vocables a parody of the French phonemic range, its middle syllables the *na-na* sound of an idiot or an infant. The voice which speaks the exhilarating words *patrie* and *citoyenne* is also the voice that sounds like the cry of a brute. The mockery of characterizing that voice as belonging to one who is "un peu beau parleur" prefigures the general devaluation of political eloquence after the grenadier's outburst.

In fact, the prologue's introductory pages are arranged so as to furnish a double gloss on their language, the second component contradicting the first. Despite early indications that historical meaning is to be preferred, the text ultimately demonstrates that historically limited interpretation is egregiously, tragically incorrect. On presenting the Fléchard family, the novel dramatically reverses the order of importance previously assigned referential and natural language.

The preliminary hierarchy culminated in the oxymoronic sequence ("Solitude, donc défiance") which embodied the unique method of understanding demanded by a unique historical situation. That sequence itself prepares a one-sentence paragraph on the reasons for the precautions: "Une embuscade était probable" (p. 8). Things are not what they seem, signs do not have their habitual meaning. In its denotation of menacingly concealed significance, *embuscade* is a one-word summary of how sense is being assigned.

The history of 1793 is the history of war. Accordingly, the martial code appears as a variant of the historical code throughout *Quatrevingt-Treize*. The short paragraph highlighting "ambush" triggers a profusion of military language whose accumulation confirms that the only real opposition between times of war and moments of pastoral is that the former lurk hidden behind the latter. Previously, "les oiseaux gazouillaient au-dessus des bayonettes" (p. 7), and a bucolic passage could interrupt narration of a military patrol. Now that the omnipresence of martial significance has been specified, martial language assumes overt prominence. The soldiers sense an enemy presence and dispose themselves for an attack. Simultaneously, lexical choices with varying generic associations disappear and military terms dominate unbrokenly. In rapid succession appear words like *grenadiers, éclaireurs, en avant, troupe, vivandière, avant-gardes, officiers, fusils braqués, couché en joue, soldats, le doigt sur la détente, mitrailler, commandement du sergent*. Narrative and lexicon combine in a sequence whose logical conclusion is the command to "Fire!"

Yet that command appears only as an unvoiced potential. The sequence does not conclude as expected. for when the Parisians discover a mother and

children where they expected an enemy, the text's lexical organization under-
goes another shift.

> Cependant la vivandière s'était hasardée à regarder à travers les broussailles, et,
> au moment où le sergent allait crier: Feu! cette femme cria: Halte! ... [D]ans une
> sorte de trou de branches, espèce de chambre de feuillage, entr'ouverte comme une
> alcôve, une femme était assise sur la mousse, ayant au sein un enfant qui tétait et
> sur les genoux les deux têtes blondes de deux enfants endormis.
> C'était là l'embuscade. (p. 9)

The second use of *embuscade*, again with the impact of a one-sentence paragraph, ridicules the hermeneutic implications of the first. Previously, what
appeared to be the glories of springtime were shown to signify a military
threat. Now what appeared to be a military threat is revealed as innocence and
love. The reader had been invited to approach the text as the soldiers approached
the forest, seeking a hidden meaning created by 1793. Now that approach
seems silly. The soldiers' quest for historical significance almost produced the
tragic conversion of blond heads into bloody skulls.

Introduction of the Fléchards combines for the first time the basic components of pastoral discourse: nature and children. The text reverts to the
supposedly nonpertinent language of springtime idyls, even repeating several
words (*mousse, branches, feuillage*) from the flowery interpolation quoted
above. Moreover, those terms are now juxtaposed to words heavy with an
idealized vision of the nuclear family's members and sanctuaries—"chambre,"
"au sein un enfant qui tétait," "les deux têtes blondes de deux enfants
endormis." *Cependant*, the first word in the first chapter's narration of the
family's discovery, is the key word from the last chapter's title. In both cases,
it introduces an unrelenting representational contrast whose conclusion is the
validation of pastoral over historical codes. In the prologue, the meaning
process which produces *ou on en a eu* as signifiers also threatens horrendously
mistaken interpretations on the level of the signified. If we take it as metalingual commentary, the beginning of *Quatrevingt-Treize* first makes a set of
decoding rules obvious and then, just as obviously, breaks them all.

Discovery of Michelle Fléchard is of course the start of the confrontation
between the soldiers' historically specific language and her ability to attach
significance only to the eternal, universal human experiences of birth,
suffering, toil, and death. The text which presents the dialogue contains an
intriguingly consistent lexical opposition which vividly illustrates the extent
to which *Quatrevingt-Treize* employs verbal structure to make its thematic
points. In order to discuss that opposition, it is necessary to outline one theory
of how verbal structure is entered in the mental dictionary, the semantic
features hypothesis.

All semantic theoreticians agree that the staggering amount of information
we store about lexical items must be organized in some manner more efficient

than discrete entries for each word. Semantic feature theory assumes that this organization is structured by minimal units of significance below the level of the word. For example, rather than making four separate entries for the four words *man, woman, boy, girl*, we remember their meanings as different combinations of the three features of humanity, adulthood, and maleness: [+human] [±adult] [±male]. The principal value of that hypothesis is that the redundancy of information it involves brings our ability to retain semantic knowledge more in line with the limits of human memory than can be the case if meaning is discretely stored. Instead of having to recall that *soldier* means [+human] [+adult] [+male] [+military], we store it as *man* plus a military feature.

The last example was chosen with a purpose. Since "93 est la guerre" (p. 135), the text consistently marks the military feature as historical. The profusion of [+military] terms which heralds the prologue's assumption of a representational schema dominated by historicity is congruent with the fact that characters who act historically are designated *only* by words containing the military feature. The members of the Red Cap battalion are *soldats, officiers, sergents, vivandières*, and *éclaireurs*, but they are not simply *men* and *women*. This fact becomes blatant during Michelle Fléchard's interrogation, when the dialogue's narrative frame darkens the line of demarcation between those who speak the words of a particular age and she who assigns meaning by a different process. Michelle Fléchard's interrogators are never named by any word without the military feature. Her own designations, potentially valid for her sex as a whole, are the historically vacuous *femme, mère*, and *veuve*. Michelle is not even referred to as a "peasant," too politically weighty in a text where *pays* and *patrie* not only summarize the Vendée war but also furnish two derivatives, *paysans* and *patriotes*, which encode the division between the war's two sides (p. 240).

The thematic contrast between historical resonance and timeless simplicity is thus underscored by a verbal barrier between the text's designations of Republican and maternal speakers. Counting up words usually leads to tedium instead of enlightenment, but in this case quantification permits succinct inscription of a critical semantic distinction sustained over twelve pages of text. The frame of the dialogue calls Michelle Fléchard *femme* eighteen times, *mère* nine times, and *veuve* twice. Her interlocutors are a *sergent* (32 occurrences), a *vivandière* (21), *soldats* (10), and *grenadiers* (9). The universal presence of a military feature inserts all the Parisians' names into a single lexical corpus here marked historically. With equal consistency, the semantic content of Michelle's designations encapsulates her inability to be conceptualized through categories subject to historical alteration.

To my knowledge, no one has ever accused Victor Hugo of being lexically uninventive. It consequently seems legitimate to posit a compelling purpose behind the prologue's monotonously repeating the same few words dozens of times. As used here, the minimal unit [+military] makes a global comment on historical engagement, for the revolutionaries' humanity never acquires textual presence as a word foregrounding the human semantic core of *man* or *woman*. Republican names convey the idea that human capacities are applied to historical purposes, armed struggle for a new society. This semantic addition to a human base also implies a development into something other than humanity. "Le soldat a un œil dans le dos" (p. 6), the prologue informs us, and the words it attaches to soldiers reiterate that suggestion of deformation. Michelle Fléchard's names universalize her as insistently as the soldiers' specify their historical engagement. A woman and a mother, she enters *Quatrevingt-Treize* as the lexicon of Hugo's contemporaries' meditations on the sex. The words applied to her weave a verbal equivalent to the iconographic message conveyed by her introduction with a baby at her breast and two children asleep on her lap.

So radical a severance makes particularly interesting the Fléchards' ultimate absorption into the Red Cap battalion. What makes possible the assimilation of the family by a group whose every textual characteristic presents its members as alien to the beings they adopt as their own? To answer that question about events at the end of the nondialogue, it is necessary to look at the structure preparing the beginning. The prologue's shift from a style dominated by military terminology to the pastoral language introducing widow and orphans has as its fulcrum the vivandière's discovery of who is actually behind the bushes: "au moment où le sergent allait crier: Feu! cette femme cria: Halte!" (p. 9). The two commands in that sentence, one choked off, the other voiced, make radically different use of their military associations. The unspoken "Fire!" is the logical conclusion of the preceding narrative and the expected culmination of the vocabulary which recounts it. On the other hand, the vivandière's "Halt!" aborts the narrative sequence and introduces a contradictory vocabulary. The militarily marked "Halt!" thus has the narrative function of terminating a military operation and the stylistic position of an announcement that military terms are no longer pertinent. Simultaneously, and for the only time in the prologue, a historical agent is given an ahistorical name: the vivandière is called a *femme*. For a brief moment, one of the Revolution's emissaries transcends military appelations, and the military connotations of what she says are irrelevant to the message she conveys.

Even though the mother's political interrogation immediately reestablishes it, this introductory annihilation of the distinction between historical and transhistorical verbal forms prefigures the dialogue's conclusion. When the Republicans' political suspicions vanish and their human compassion awakens, the marks of their separation from the family undergo a stunning reversal of value. The sergeant's mustache, for instance, was imagistically associated with the historical language terrifying Michelle Fléchard. Prominent when identification of the Red Cap battalion caused the mother to shake from head to foot (p. 10), the sergeant's mustache is an essential feature of the "moue militaire" (p. 18) he assumes for interrogation. Yet when the baby smiles at the sergeant, his awesome mustache becomes something wholly different: "l'on vit une grosse larme rouler sur sa joue et s'arrêter au bout de sa moustache comme une perle" (p. 20). Immediately prior to that teary cleansing, the gulf between Breton and Parisian speech, earlier so momentous, is revealed to be inconsequential. The mother says that she and her children spent the night in an *émousse*, which, as the sergeant explains to his men, is the local word for a hollow tree trunk. The sergeant then asserts that this sort of dialectical difference is unimportant —"ils ne sont pas forcés d'être de Paris" (p. 20)—and gives his own version of pastoral fascination with nature and children's togetherness. The family's night in the *émousse* gave a material form to the ideal union of all God's creatures in one, and "ça devait être drôle d'entendre un arbre crier: *Papa, maman!*" (p. 20).

Definitive neutralization of historical language occurs in the prologue's final lines, when the revolutionaries' adoption of a timeless ethic generates a timeless code banishing the previous sense of historical words. The pearly tear on his mustache, the sergeant raised his voice.

> —Camarades, de tout ça je conclus que le bataillon va devenir père. Est-ce convenu? Nous adoptons ces trois enfants-là.
> —Vive la République! crièrent les grenadiers.
> —C'est dit, fit le sergent.
> Et il étendit les deux mains au-dessus de la mère et des enfants.
> —Voilà, dit-il, les enfants du bataillon du Bonnet Rouge.
> La vivandière sauta de joie.
> —Trois têtes dans un bonnet, cria-t-elle.
> Puis elle éclata en sanglots, embrassa éperdument la pauvre veuve et lui dit:
> —Comme la petite a déjà l'air gamine!
> —Vive la République! répétèrent les soldats.
> Et le sergent dit à la mère:
> —Venez, citoyenne. (pp. 20-21)

The stylistic fields established by that passage in effect excise the historical content of words which had previously functioned as key markers of the historical vision. The lexical transformation *Vendéenne → mère* was an implicit effect of the family's discovery by the soldiers, whose efforts to impose the reverse transformation by defining the mother politically came to nothing. Their frustration leads to an identical removal of the military feature from their own designation, this one explicit in the sergeant's announcement that "le *bataillon* va devenir *père*" (p. 20). In that striking sentence, the soldiers' acceptance of ahistorical duties earns for them a name which triumphantly removes the vaguely inhuman impression created by the military seme omnipresent in their previous designations.

Assumption of paternity also removes the historical content of *Vive la République*, an archetypically political affirmation which in this passage is

first a formula for adoption and next a paraphrase for "Kitchy-kitchy-koo."
As will be the case when the novel's final chapter depicts Gauvain joining the
phrase *Vive la République* to acts certain to harm the Republic, the first
chapter rigorously excludes the possibility of interpreting the Great Revolution's
cry as in any way pertinent to the Revolution. The sergeant's epigrammatic
response to his men's first shout (*C'est dit* literally means "It is said.") is an
eloquent reminder that *what* is said is personal not collective, human rather
than political. The ringing shout of historical creation introduces sublimely
ahistorical deeds: "And he spread both his hands above mother and children."

"Enfants du bataillon du Bonnet-Rouge" both reiterates the *bataillon* → *père*
transformation and neutralizes another sign formerly heavy with historical
meaning. Hugo's prologue had emphasized the red cap's association with
rebellion by placing the Red Cap battalion at momentous upheavals like
August 10 and January 21. The first humiliated the Old Regime, the second
exterminated it, and the battalion's presence at both (p. 16) binds those
given the name of the sans-culotte symbol with the revolutionary fervor that
prompted its most exuberant outpourings. Yet the red cap is also submerged
in the rising sea of familial sentiment which concludes the first chapter. The
Thermidorian reaction combatted the rebellious spirit concretized in the red
cap by rebaptizing the Bonnet-Rouge section with the reassuring name of a
compass point. More skillful, *Quatrevingt-Treize* retains the sign but changes
its sense from public fury to private comfort. The Revolution's red cap
becomes a paternal night cap capable of containing several children; "trois
têtes dans un bonnet" is an image appropriate to the new responsibilities of the
battalion become a father, as the joyous leaps punctuating the phrase are
suited to a change in mission from seeking the Republic's enemies to aiding
widows and orphans.

The final words in the prologue magisterially complete its emasculation of
historical signs. Although the opposition between words containing the military
feature and those with purely human semes has been maintained through more
than a hundred occurrences of the two lexical classes in prose framing a conversation, "et le sergent dit à la mère" is the *first* sentence to join nouns from
both classes with a verb denoting communication. Since this suggestion that
speech is finally replacing noise coincides with introduction of the historically
marked *citoyenne*, it might seem that the final common language is historical.
In fact, however, the text does not permit the revolutionary title to convey
revolutionary meaning, and the prologue concludes with pastoral stasis exu-
berantly dominant. In *Venez, citoyenne*, the first word neutralizes the political
appelation which is the second, for the *vous* form of address is a
synecdoche of a discourse alien to that which made everyone a citizen. "If
vous goes with Monsieur, *toi* goes with citizen."[13] The same thrust toward
liberty, equality, and fraternity which abolished titles also excluded singular
vous, considered the obsequious second-person equivalent of the royal *nous*.

The Revolution's militants were known as *tutoyeurs*, and they began to impose their preferred form of address at the same time as their preferred form of government, after the world-historical day of August 10. Although their success was never complete, *tu* did become so general that the standard formula for concluding citizens' letters to public officials was *ton égal en droits*. (Having had to struggle, like many of my compatriots, with ponderous French equivalents of "Sincerely yours" like *Veuillez agréer, monsieur, l'expression de mes sentiments les plus distingués*, I find that particular usage marvelously congenial.) In 1793, a delegation from Parisian popular societies, convinced that "the principles of our language must be as dear to us as the laws of our Republic," apostrophized the Convention on the intimate bond between singular *vous* and "fanaticism, pride and feudalism."[14] The rules of the societies that delegation represented are exemplified in this excerpt: "Members will treat one another as brothers, use *tu* with one another and call one another citizens."[15] One could multiply the evidence, but the crucial point should already be clear: the sergeant's words to the mother join a revolutionary noun to a counterrevolutionary verb.

The prologue's construction makes full textual use of the extratextual fact that its two last words evoke contrary political positions. The original discovery of a family where an enemy was expected momentarily distracts attention from the Republicans' historical purpose and produces the unique designation of the vivandière as a woman. During that interlude, the sergeant also emerges from his historical matrix and uses *vous* to address his prisoner. When he begins his political interrogation, however, he immediately adopts the correct political form and employs the egalitarian *tu*, a form continued until he. and his comrades decide to become a father. That decision demands a more reverential attitude toward their children's mother, one which political formulas are incapable of expressing. The vivandière, whose historical commitment is tempered by human compassion, never fails to address the mother as *vous*; the sergeant ultimately joins her in implicit recognition that the transhistorical sanctity of parenthood is so great that no historical imperative can refute its right to the form of address which best conveys respect. As was the case with *bonnet rouge, vive la République*, and military terms, the prologue's last paragraphs constitute a context which effectively dehistoricizes the quintessential revolutionary title. The chapter's conclusion reverses the meaning of historical signs as systematically as its beginning refuted the implications of pastoral language.

To summarize the metalingual commentary which is the prologue, *Quatre-vingt-Treize* begins by presenting distinct and distinctive ways of meaning, one grounded in the French Revolution, the other pointing away from history. Each representational system imposes global decoding procedures which, as dramatized in the nondialogue between mother and Republicans, are incompatible with those of the other. Signs' meaning depends absolutely on the code in which they figure, a basic fact first made apparent when a forest filled with spring flowers is interpreted as a battleground filled with enemy armies. The converse of this historical alteration of pastoral imagery occurs in the prologue's final paragraphs, where the language of the Revolution conveys a transhistorical family message. To read any part of this novel, it is first necessary to determine contextual identification of the code in which it is written.

Revolutionary signification depends on the meaning created by revolutionary action. *Patrie* and *pays* summarize the Vendée war not simply because of a featural difference in semantic content but also because their opposition evokes a historically specific, collective will to implement *patrie*'s additional feature in the world by "giving Frenchmen a *patrie*." On the other hand, the signs of nature's endless cycles and humanity's timeless duties overtly proclaim their status as units of a mental structure without connection to a material universe. Their semantic force derives from their sempiternal use to convey sempiternal concepts instead of from men making new concepts and seeking commensurate forms of expression. Like the top half of the picture illustrating the report on the Terror, pastoral signs exist in a purely semiotic realm where images speak to images. Like the picture as a whole, historical signs convey meaning inseparable from consciousness of the events which are history.

The first chapter of *Quatrevingt-Treize* not only illustrates the indefeasibility of its required interpretive processes. More importantly, it establishes a clear moral hierarchy for the disparate representational systems it employs. When pastoral signs are understood historically, the result is very nearly a tragic slaughter of the innocent; when an attempt is made to engage a mother in political discourse, the result is *ou on en a eu*. The play on *embuscade*, whose first occurrence urges a quest for hidden historical significance and whose second contemptuously ridicules such a quest, encapsulates the prologue's overall development. To historicize the ahistorical is to descend to egregious misunderstandings and incoherent babblings.

The situation is quite different when a pastoral message integrates historical signs by stripping them of their historical specificity. The prologue finally uses the Revolution's new words not to name new things but to express what is as old as mankind. *Vive la République* is "said" to display paternal delight rather than to exhort political struggle. The text's preference for the Republican party in the Vendée conflict is apparent neither in the exhilarating words which the Red Cap battalion brings to the victim of the Old Regime nor in the vigorous rhetoric those words punctuate. Revolutionary eloquence is declared to be incongruous, revolutionary words do not communicate. Textual validation of the language of 1793 comes only when it affirms an ethic predating it by millennia, the moral code that Gauvain also set above royalty and revolution: "l'immense attendrissement de l'âme humaine, la protection due aux faibles . . . la paternité due à tous les enfants" (p. 442). The mother does not earn the right to be called a *citoyenne*. Rather the revolutionary earns the right to use his word by respecting motherhood sufficiently to address its representative with counterrevolutionary deference.

The prologue's beginning evokes "Gabriel Péri" and the words that give life because there are lives that give meaning. Its conclusion evokes not Eluard but Claude Roy's poem on the multiple ways of making the same old statement. The soldiers of the Red Cap battalion ultimately speak the words of social combat and historical change only to affirm a commitment to love and life which is outside history and beyond societies.

> Je dis toujours la même chose
> la vie l'amour la mort le temps.

5

Can a Good Deed Be a Bad Deed?

The remainder of Hugo's novel develops from a variant—"Au printemps de 1793" (p. 22)—of the opening which the prologue continually glosses, "Dans les derniers jours de mai 1793." The novel further repeats the prologue when it demonstrates that adopting a set of interpretive procedures is implicit assumption of one moral stance and rejection of others. Lantenac's metamorphosis is prefigured by the Red Cap battalion's education on how to respond to children and flowers. Gauvain's meditation on Lantenac's new meaning is prepared by the first chapter's dehistoricization of historical signs.

There is nevertheless a major distinction between the prologue and the text as a whole, which eventually rejects the idea that it is possible to integrate pastoral and historical visions of the world. Unlike the Red Cap battalion, Gauvain and Lantenac are required to betray their historical mission when they accept another kind of duty. Analogously, the last chapter's isolation of pastoral purity from historical perfidy is unnecessary in the first chapter, where the mother is a citizeness, the battalion becomes a father, and erroneously historical interpretation of nature is ephemeral. Whereas the prologue does realize Hugo's ambition to "cast a calming light" on historical signs, the following pages consign history to endless darkness.

The progressive elaboration of its antihistorical stance, one of the most fascinating aspects of *Quatrevingt-Treize*, derives from increasing realization that there is no refuge from history within human time. The prologue's soldiers, without acting *against* their party, nevertheless act *for* humanity. In contrast, the protagonists can respond to moral imperatives only by recanting political choices. In the prologue, characters can be both historically and ethically luminous; by the conclusion, one form of virtue repels the other. The light of Gauvain's soul finally cannot radiate through the garb of a political leader.

The prologue's adoption of a counterrevolutionary second-person form to address a woman named by a revolutionary title is a prophetic suggestion of the contradiction between historical and timeless speech which will perplex the text until its concluding assertion that all historical signs are as vile as the guillotine. Finally, the transient language of revolutionary change cannot be reconciled with pastoral's eternal certainty. The dilemma is this: *if history is meaningful, then meaning is historical*. The novel's efforts to avoid the conclusion despite its forceful assertion of the proposition leads to a retreat above the realm where history can mean anything at all.

The need for a retreat becomes overt when the story line which takes over after the prologue brings Lantenac into contact with Tellmarch. Arriving from England to take general command of the Vendée rebellion, Lantenac learns that his Republican enemies, informed of his supposedly secret plans, have aroused the countryside to search for him and offered an enormous reward for his capture. Immediately after this discovery, he is recognized by Tellmarch, a beggar who, despite his reasons for hating the lord of the region where he has long been sunk in poverty and despite the fortune he could earn by a denunciation, not only keeps silent but shelters Lantenac for the night. On leaving Tellmarch's cave, Lantenac assumes leadership of a band of Royalists to order that Republican prisoners be slaughtered and the village which quartered them burnt. Tellmarch, his saintly deed the source of hellish savagery, bitterly learns that what he thought was the compassionate salvation of a man was in fact the thoughtless release of a brute.

Tellmarch is a pivotal figure in *Quatrevingt-Treize*. Although identified with both the novel's representatives of transhistorical values, Gauvain and Michelle Fléchard, his function in the chronicle of historical conflict sharply contests humanistic ethics. Tellmarch's identification with the mother begins immediately after his introduction. Michelle's failure to respond to questions like "Es-tu des bleus? Es-tu des blancs?" followed this original assessment of her: "C'est une pauvre" (p. 11). Tellmarch responds to "Etes-vous républicain? Etes-vous royaliste?" with an identical assessment of himself: "Je suis un pauvre" (p. 98).

Tellmarch's announcement of the impoverishment and resultant political indifference which Michelle embodies exemplifies the major distinction between the two allegorical figures. Although they represent the same order of values, the inarticulate mother does so unknowingly, the beggar with highly conscious eloquence. Michelle's restriction to a pastoral universe was implicit in her existence as a creature of the forest and her deafness to historical language. Tellmarch's concern with natural cycles and neglect of political progressions is explicit. Interested only in the sun rising and the moon waxing and waning (p. 101), Tellmarch lives below ground; history takes place above, where "on va, on vient, il se passe des choses; moi, je suis là sous les étoiles" (p. 102). Michelle's sublimity appears as unthinking deeds like giving her children all the food the soldiers offer the starving family because "elle est la mère" (p. 18). Tellmarch's sublimity is vocal as well as gestural. His decision to rescue Lantenac produces a speech almost too noble to bear. "En vous voyant, je me suis dit: Quand je pense que quelqu'un qui livrerait cet homme-ci gagnerait soixante mille francs et ferait sa fortune! Dépêchons-nous de le cacher" (p. 99).

Yet, despite their paradigmatic identity, syntagmatically Michelle is exalted and Tellmarch degraded. The beggar's response to human misery leads to political violation of the family, nature, the home, and life itself. Not only do Tellmarch's actions make the massacre of Herbe-en-Pail possible, his words make it inevitable; he informed the White general that the village had not resisted the Blues (p. 96). Michelle figures maternity, whose transcendent excellence the text illuminates. Tellmarch embodies ideals no less sanctified, compassion and honesty, *caritas* and *veritas*, but his virtues cause carnage. Where the prologue seemed to offer a pastoral escape, the rest of Part I encloses characters in a political world from which escape is inconceivable. While living under the stars, while watching the sun rise and the moon wane, Tellmarch became a figure crucial to the course of a world-historical war.

Symbolically equated to Michelle Fléchard, Tellmarch is more concretely identified with Gauvain, who also rescues the marquis de Lantenac. Both characters are led by their high ethical standards to keep from harm the brutal enemy of all that ethics implies. Tellmarch learns the consequences of saving Lantenac as he walks through the burning houses of Herbe-en-Pail and finds massacred prisoners and women victims of the firing squad. The result of Gauvain's rescue of Lantenac will be identical: "les maisons brûlées, les prisonniers massacrés . . . les femmes fusillées" (p. 440). The only difference is that Tellmarch has the excuse of ignorance. His repeated "Si j'avais su" (pp. 120, 278) implies that foreknowledge would have made him act differently, whereas Gauvain is fully aware that his action will increase the number of Lantenac's innocent victims. Yet Gauvain is the novel's moral exemplar, Tellmarch at best its holy fool. Part of the reason is that five pages of desolation hammer home Tellmarch's responsibility while the crimes Gauvain makes possible appear as abstract predictions. This difference is itself the effect of a global transformation effected by the novel's definitive assumption of its thematic orientation. Tellmarch's exclusive concern with the rising sun is obscene as he walks from horror to horror; Gauvain becomes one with the rising sun in a chapter that repeatedly announces how magnificent he is to do so.

Echoes of Tellmarch's delineation therefore appear to radically different effect during Gauvain's apotheosis. The beggar attends only to flowers, birds, and trees in a region "en pleine guerre, en pleine conflagration" (p. 276). Gauvain's world too is "en pleine guerre sociale, en pleine conflagration" (p. 432), but he ignores havoc to enter eternal light by performing the same deed for which Tellmarch was plunged into gloom. Tellmarch voices his political unconcern in statements like this: "Je ne m'en mêle pas. Les événements sont les événements" (p. 101). His involvement in slaughter makes it doubtful that he continues to perceive all events as tautologically identical, a transformation reversed when Gauvain progresses from engagement in events to contemplation of his inner self. The speculative "Que me font les événements, si j'ai ma conscience?" (p. 479) follows Gauvain's recognition that "lorsque les événements, qui sont variables, nous font une question, la justice, qui est immuable, nous somme de répondre" (p. 431). Tellmarch develops from belief that events are events to awareness of the awesome distinctions among them. Gauvain's awareness that events are changeable underlies his decision to cling to an ideal that is not.

When Tellmarch learns that his compassion, by rights as immutable as Gauvain's justice, is in fact criminally variable, his anguish predicts the existentialist thesis that political responsibility is an inescapable part of the human condition. To use a parallel more nearly contemporary with *Quatrevingt-Treize*, Tellmarch could fit into Vallès's *Insurgé*, which contains this memorably brief discussion of engagement: " 'I've never been mixed up in politics.' 'That's why I'm killing you.' "[1] On the other hand, situational ethics are unthinkable within the Gauvain-Lantenac narrative, so resolutely essentialist that Plato comes immediately to mind. Like Socrates before Diotima, Gauvain perceives "a nature which in the first place is everlasting, not growing and decaying, or waxing or waning; secondly, not fair in one point of view and foul in another, or at one time and in one relation or at one place fair, at another time and in another relation and in another place foul, as if fair to some and foul to others."[2] Seen through the historical situation in which the novel places Tellmarch, virtue is indeed fair in one relation and foul in another. Viewed in the realm of everlasting truth which Gauvain attains, that virtue acquires the beauteous permanence of Ideas and requires Plato's ascendent imagery for its expression: "Au-dessus du sombre duel entre le faux et le relatif, dans les profondeurs, la face de la vérité avait tout à coup apparu" (p. 433).

The massacre of Herbe-en-Pail made even the family an affliction: " 'Comme on remercie Dieu dans ces moments-là de n'avoir pas de famille!' " (p. 118). Gauvain triumphantly sets the family back in its rightful place, implicitly in going back into the family rather than remaining in civil war (p. 438), explicitly in defining his duty. "La lutte des passions bonnes et des passions mauvaises faisait en ce moment sur le monde le chaos . . . c'était à Gauvain maintenant d'en dégager la famille" (p. 443).

The capacity of "ce moment" and "ces moments" to cloud the splendor of justice and the family is of course the threat posed by historical signification in general. History, chaos in the world, develops meaning systems in which even the most radiant signifiers convey pernicious signifieds. Tellmarch offers to save Lantenac on condition that the aristocrat has not come "pour faire le mal," to which Lantenac's response is unequivocal. "Je viens ici pour faire le bien" (p. 103). Although absolutely sincere in speaking thus, Lantenac defines good and evil by a process Tellmarch cannot accept, that which equates "bien" with restoration of France's former social system. Lantenac's historical good is thus timeless evil. Conversely, the timeless good in Tellmarch's generosity produces the historical evil of a peaceful village's destruction. Fair is foul and foul is fair.

The weird sisters' oxymoronic language is appropriate to discussion of Tellmarch, whose cruelly awakened historical consciousness demolishes the presupposition of semantic stability obvious when he had Lantenac promise to do good. If good and evil mean different things from different historical perspectives, then there is nothing to prevent them from becoming synonyms instead of opposites. "Une bonne action peut donc être une mauvaise action" (p. 278). When words cannot be trusted, the morality and logic whose rules they encode vanish, as is continually apparent in the novel's play with the lexical identity of good and evil. For Lantenac, "en guerre civile, c'est la *pire* qui est la *meilleure*. La *bonté* d'une guerre se juge à la quantité de *mal* qu'elle fait" (p. 83). For his fellow Royalists, *bon* and *féroce* are interchangeable (p. 37). On the other side, Marat sees mercy as a fault (p. 174), an opinion shared by Cimourdain (p. 274), who also believes that history redefines all other virtues as well: "Dans des temps comme les nôtres, la *pitié* peut être une des formes de la *trahison*" (p. 289).

Although they do not always acquire a surface realization, temporal phrases like Cimourdain's "dans des temps comme les nôtres" or Lantenac's "en guerre civile" are invariably the underlying cause of sentences which manifestly proclaim such violations of morality, logic, and language. Accordingly, when Gauvain finds a refuge above his time, lexical distortions disappear. If Tellmarch learns that good deeds can be bad deeds, Gauvain teaches that good deeds are always and everywhere the same. Because he was captured "en pleine bonne action" (p. 436), Lantenac must not be punished. Although one "bonne action" hid a hundred "actions criminelles" (p. 462) from Gauvain, his behavior toward his enemy at least guarantees that the two categories do not get mixed up with one another. As Radoub says, if you guillotine people because of their "bonne action," then you just don't know where you are any more (p. 465). Gauvain's ascent takes him above the confusion of good and evil to a realm where you know very well where you are.

Historical meaning is that form of signification in which extralinguistic activity infiltrates semantic structure. Although acceptable for words like *patrie* and *bonnet rouge*, this invasion becomes diabolical when it attacks good and evil. Signs whose purity ought to be apparent in the textual character of self-defining, self-generating units of a self-contained system in fact point outward as insistently as referential language. The novel's introductory opposition between Brittany and Paris was legitimately specific to a historical moment. But Tellmarch's good deed should be safer from historical mutation than the names of Parisian sections. *Ci-devant* kings and nobles are one thing, *ci-devant* virtue something else.

By displaying the perils of transhistorical behavior in a style redefining words that add historical content to a human semantic core, Tellmarch's narrative further refutes the prologue. Original designation of Parisian revolutionaries exclusively by words which include both the feature [+human] and the feature [+military] suggested that the second feature was added to, not amalgamated with, the first. When the historical agents' humanity appeared in their transhistorical treatment of widow and children, historical content was stripped from their names to reveal that what was [+historical] was also [+human].

Tellmarch's encounter with Lantenac challenges that identity by a contradictory development of historical and human words.

> Un homme était là dans les haies, de haute taille comme lui, vieux comme lui, comme lui en cheveux blancs, et plus en haillons encore que lui-même. Presque son pareil.
> Cet homme s'appuyait sur un long bâton.
> L'homme reprit. . . . (p. 95)

Although physically Lantenac's twin, Tellmarch's lexical presence severs him from the Royalist as irretrievably as the prologue separates mother from revolutionaries. This beggar is human not historical, as is evident in the presentation's repetitive *un homme, cet homme, l'homme. Homme*, identical to the prologue's *femme* in its historical vacuousness, will designate Tellmarch thirteen times in the frame the text supplies for his dialogue with Lantenac. His other names—"mendiant," "pauvre," and the personal proper noun "Tellmarch" —are varied in form but alike in rejection of historically specific meaning. Even "mendiant" and "pauvre" lose their social connotations when Tellmarch disclaims all interest in the quarrels between rich and poor (p. 101).

Lantenac's designation is as rigid and historical as his interlocutor's are supple and human. He is named by the single word *marquis*, repeated nineteen times in the nine pages describing his meeting with Tellmarch. This lexical opposition is often starkly set out in short sentences like "Le *marquis* considérait cet *homme*" (p. 98) or "Le *marquis* se mit à interroger cet *homme*" (p. 100). Tellmarch originally has a textual presence whose human sense is as certain as the fact that a good deed is a good deed; afterwards, he acquires a lexical form as problematic as the equation of good and evil. From "entendant peut-être le bruit des hommes, mais écoutant le chant des oiseaux" (p. 114), Tellmarch erupts into awareness that he is responsible for the most cacophonic noise men can make. Seeing smoke, he walks to its source and finds the homes laid waste and the bodies laid out by his noble compassion. The narrative of his walk through the chamber of horrors he has built refers to him 'with only one word, "Tellmarch." Since proper names do not have normal semantic content, the beggar's new designation is as indeterminate as his behavior. *Marquis* appeared as Lantenac's invariant designation nineteen times in nine pages; *Tellmarch* appears nineteen times in five pages, a compressed invariant that repeatedly suggests the altered significance of the character who was a man and became a meaning yet to be assigned.

Tellmarch rescues the wounded Michelle Fléchard and uses his mysterious skills to cure her. This compassion toward an ahistorical figure partly redeems

him—"avoir sauvé cette *mère* le consola d'avoir sauvé ce *marquis*" (p. 278)—
and he regains the historically immaculate label *homme*. Nevertheless, Tellmarch
ponders his contact with Lantenac as a lesson in historical semantics as well
as historical morality. "Marquis" includes the feature [+rank], highly charged
during the revolutionary struggle for liberty, equality, and fraternity, and the
presence of this additional feature challenges the sense of the word's [+human]
foundation. Hierarchically ordered semantic features can be serially removed to
produce a logical progression from subordinate to superordinate categories.
For example, the statement that a soldier or a marquis is also a man is semantically the removal of a terminal feature and the lexical realization of the
remaining string. Whereas the prologue's humanization of the Red Cap soldiers
effects the first of these progressions, Tellmarch's experience makes him
contest the second's legitimacy.

> Et il se demandait: —Mais alors pourquoi ai-je sauvé ce seigneur?
> Et il se répondait: —Parce que c'est un homme.
> Il fut là-dessus quelque temps pensif, et il reprit en lui-même: —En suis-je bien
> sûr? (p. 277)

Reformulating the problem of meaning constantly posed by historical signification in *Quatrevingt-Treize*, Tellmarch first refers to Lantenac as a *seigneur*,
like *marquis* in adding a marker of social rank to a human semantic base.
"Parce que c'est un *homme*" excises the historical feature and executes the
surface form of the human remainder. The final doubt, however, challenges the
correctness of that perfectly straightforward operation. As existence in history
makes it impossible to act on purely human motives, so historically modeled
semantics invalidates the human significance of human words. Tellmarch's
doubt is an instance of the major theme of *Quatrevingt-Treize*: the meanings
created by historical action corrupt all other kinds.

The novel often reaffirms the error of assuming that one can progress from
the lexical realization of [+human] [+historical] to that of [+human] alone.
Discussion of the revolutionary turmoil in Paris, for instance, incorporates
these historical quotations: "Un *roi* mort n'est pas un *homme* de moins"
(p. 191); "J'ai en horreur l'effusion du sang *humain*, mais le sang d'un *roi*
n'est pas le sang d'un *homme*. La mort" (p. 198). Within revolutionary semantics, humanity does not subtend signs to which all other signifying systems
accord a human base.

Hence the necessity of transcending revolutionary semantics, as is done
when Lantenac's nobility teaches Gauvain that "au-dessus de l'absolu *révolutionnaire*, il y a l'absolu *humain*" (p. 431). The mental debate leading the
Republican general to renounce struggle for the Republic constantly refutes
Tellmarch's doubts about whether or not historical circumstances leave
humanity intact. Not only does he continually name Lantenac a man, but

Gauvain also perceives the marquis's metamorphosis into a human being as figuring the emergence of humanity itself from the conflict concealing it. "Un Lantenac inattendu entrait en scène. Un héros sortait du monstre; plus qu'un héros, un *homme*" (p. 437); "[Lantenac] rentrait dans *l'humanité*" (p. 435); "*l'humanité* avait vaincu *l'inhumain*" (p. 432); "Lantenac venait de rentrer dans *l'humanité*" (p. 438); "Lantenac, dominant ce chaos, venait d'en dégager *l'humanité*" (p. 443). For Gauvain, Lantenac stands in two relations to humanity. He is both the individual penitent taken back into something beyond him and the great liberator who himself frees that something from chaos. Analogously, Lantenac's textual designations have a double function. The vagaries of the [+human] feature in his name both describe his personal character and embody the novel's global commentary on humanity in history.

The commentary's conclusion is of course that there is no humanity in history. Lantenac reverts to savagery, Gauvain is killed, the Fléchards vanish from the text, and radiant words like *homme* and *humain* appear only in the most dismal stylistic fields. There are actually two ways for Gauvain to emulate the glory of Lantenac attesting *humanity* despite the open jaws of civil war (p. 442). The one he chooses is to represent reality through the infantile language in which, since it can be said that civil war does not exist, humanity is inviolably safe from the teeth snapping at it. The one he rejects is to preserve humanity by ending the civil war. The novel emphasizes that the second option is indeed practically viable by repeating that Lantenac's death is the war's end: "Lui fini, la guerre civile était finie" (pp. 439-40). What makes finishing civil war inferior to saying that civil war does not exist? If historical action could also preserve humanity, why does the text have Gauvain withdraw from history and follow him on his retreat?

The answers to those questions are implicit in the contrast between Tellmarch's vacillating significance and Gauvain's unflickering radiance. The novel cannot admit meanings which alter in any way, even if the change is positive. Historical sense is man-made, the sense ultimately asserted by Gauvain is impervious to man's power to make and unmake. The basic antagonism is less between historical good and evil than between shifting and permanent good. If Gauvain must act in history to validate moral excellence, it follows that moral excellence depends on historical action. This consequence is precisely what the text must forestall, for the signifying system it affirms cannot admit connections between meaning which always is and historical creation which may not be. By not humanizing politics through elimination of the inhuman politician whose existence perpetuates civil war, Gauvain announces that humanization is an essential truth rather than an existential process. Tellmarch, within history, saves Lantenac and suffers; Gauvain, above history, saves Lantenac and becomes divine. The final chapter designates Gauvain as *archange* and *âme* (pp. 490-91), but never as *homme*. Within the vision of *Quatrevingt-Treize*, to disengage humanity from chaos is not a human activity.

Only Cimourdain is called a "man" in the concluding chapter, and the storms of 1793 have long since made Cimourdain's humanity problematic: "Un tel homme était-il un homme?" (p. 141). He was before the Revolution, when he was the adoring tutor who ignored Gauvain's claim to all [+rank] names and represented his pupil through the human *enfant* (p. 141). Out of love for that child, Cimourdain produced a change in signs and sense opposite to that which the text effects for the child's great-uncle, the marquis de Lantenac: "De ce petit *seigneur*, il avait fait un *homme*" (p. 142). The *seigneur* → *homme* deduction is not appropriate to the uncle; thanks to Cimourdain, it is chronologically as well as logically descriptive of the nephew.

But Cimourdain's 1793 understanding is uniquely historical. Introduced in the book entitled "A Paris," Cimourdain incarnates the tumult which transformed the capital. Working "à se refaire *homme*" (p. 134), the former priest made his goal unattainable by substituting the *patrie* for that which is in *Quatrevingt-Treize* the only human environment, the family (p. 134). Revolutionary ardor makes him promise to kill his spiritual son for displaying mercy to enemies of the fatherland. A constellation of family terms—*père, frère, mère, fils*—recurs in description of Cimourdain the tutor (p. 142); when Cimourdain the revolutionary agrees to execute even Gauvain, the novel refuses all such eternal words for the referential lexicon of historical situation: *ci-devant, Comité de salut public, Marat, Danton, Robespierre* (p. 175). The vocabulary shift manifests transformed understanding, Cimourdain's definitive acceptance of a historical vision.

Although Cimourdain himself does not appear in it, the first chapter in the section of the novel bearing his name is ideally suited to introducing the absolute politician. Its first sentence presents pastoral values as nostalgic counterpoints to a new society where families and nature no longer signify to the same purpose.

> On vivait en public, on mangeait sur des tables dressés devant les portes, les femmes assises sur les perrons des églises faisaient de la charpie en chantant la *Marseillaise*, le parc Monceaux et le Luxembourg étaient des champs de manœuvre, il y avait dans tous les carrefours des armureries en plein travail, on fabriquait des fusils sous les yeux des passants qui battaient des mains; on n'entendait que ce mot dans toutes les bouches: *Patience. Nous sommes en révolution.* (pp. 123-24)

That long sentence begins an eight-page paragraph, more Proustian than Hugolian in its need to include everything before concluding. The passage's failure to block words into compact sentences and paragraphs manifests the comprehensive nature of its subject, the Revolution which constituted a totality no part of which can be represented in isolation. That sacred locus of parents and children together, the family meal in the family home, vanishes when people "live in public" and eat outdoors. Rather than making cloth into clothes for their children, women shred it for their nation's soldiers while singing not a lullaby but the most stirring of calls to arms. The Monceau and Luxembourg parks, in other times bucolic havens of trees and grass, now echo to military commands and marching feet. People no longer speak to convey personal messages to other individuals, for their single utterance is designed to recall the magnitude of the revolution including them all. The presence of history entails the absence of all traditional havens against it.

In the prologue, the utterances of *bonnet rouge* made Michelle the woman tremble with terror. In revolutionary Paris, women and red caps merge into a single entity which transforms the Eternal Feminine into a historical creation: "Les femmes disaient: *Nous sommes jolies sous le bonnet rouge*" (p. 124). Children too are creatures of a time rather then embodiments of a timeless abstraction. The eight-page paragraph concludes:

> Sur tous les murs, des affiches, grandes, petites, blanches, jaunes, vertes, rouges, imprimées, manuscrites, où on lisait ce cri: *Vive la République!* Les petits enfants bégayaient *Ça ira.*
>
> Ces petits enfants, c'était l'immense avenir. (p. 130)

The last sentence constitutes a complete paragraph. Coming after one eight pages long, this six-word paragraph attains a graphic relief commensurate with its majestic subject, childhood, the value for which historical action unfolds. From what men do in society, the text proceeds to what children see in their dreams.

Or at least tries to before abandoning the attempt. Rather than continuing to describe what might be in ideal time, the novel immediately begins to recount what was in actual time, the foulness of Paris during the Thermidorian reaction. The one-sentence paragraph on an immense future dissolves into a scathing chronicle of a historical era; an "accès de folie publique" (p. 130), but nothing that could possibly accomplish the realization of little children's great hopes.

The effort to shift from Paris in 1793 to children in eternity was in fact doomed from the introductory mention of childish voices singing a revolutionary song. In order to equate the Revolution's children with mankind's hope, reference to the song which "les petits enfants bégayaient" ought to look forward to the text's later paean to children's "bégaiement" as "le cantique le plus sublime qu'on puisse entendre" (p. 329). But Paris's children, taught to sing by history, stammer not a sublime canticle but the rabid call for violent rebellion entitled *Ça ira.*

Ah! ça ira, ça ira, ça ira,
Les aristocrates à la lanterne;
Ah! ça ira, ça ira, ça ira,
Les aristocrates on les pendra;
Et quand on les aura tous pendus,
On leur fich'ra la pelle au cul.

"Les Rues de Paris dans ce temps-là" prefigures the despair of "Cependant le soleil se lève." Since what will be is corrupted by what was, there is no escape from corruption in history. Women and children should be allegories for beauty and innocence, but Hugo's depiction of revolutionary Paris begins with women singing a promise to water France's furrows with impure blood and ends with children singing a promise to stick shovels up the asses of corpses.

At the same time that it asserts this historicity of activity, however, the novel attemps to preserve certain activities from historical battery by placing them above the revolutionary turmoil: "Au-dessus des révolutions *la vérité et la justice* demeurent comme le ciel étoilé au-dessus des tempêtes" (p. 208) is one example. Another is children in the abstract, as opposed to the concrete singers of revolutionary Paris, children who are in fact identical to truth and justice. "[C]elui qui n'a pas vécu encore n'a pas fait le mal, *il est la justice, il est la vérité*, il est la blancheur, et les immenses anges du ciel sont dans les petits enfants" (p. 433).

Yet *Ça ira* is also in little children, and people who *have* lived are no more confident of the eternal meaning of justice and truth than they are of good and evil. When Tellmarch is about to discover that a good deed can be a bad deed, the novel interpolates a meditation on antithetical ways of interpreting smoke, a nonverbal signifier whose signified is uniquely the effect of circumstances.

Rien de plus doux qu'une fumée, rien de plus effrayant. Il y a les fumées paisibles et il y a les fumées scélérates. Une fumée, l'épaisseur et la couleur d'une fumée, c'est toute la différence entre la paix et la guerre, entre la fraternité et la haine, entre l'hospitalité et le sépulcre, entre la vie et la mort. Une fumée qui monte dans les arbres peut signifier ce qu'il y a de plus charmant au monde, le foyer, et ce qu'il y a de plus affreux, l'incendie; et tout le bonheur comme tout le malheur de l'homme sont parfois dans cette chose éparse au vent. (pp. 114-15)

While linguistic criticism has undoubtedly created a tendency to attach undue importance to passages containing words like *signifier*, several features authorize reading this occurrence of the verb as indicative of the novel's overall vision of meaning. The passage occurs just prior to the *homme* → *Tellmarch* transformation, the problematic semantics it introduces is fundamental to the beggar's attempt to understand what he has done, and words are like smoke in being insubstantial things "scattered by the wind" that convey nevertheless all the meanings mankind can conceive. More importantly, the pronounced indeterminacy of smoke's sense here encapsulates history's general effect on signification. What Tellmarch sees can mean either pole of a long series of contraries: *rien de plus doux / rien de plus effrayant; paisible / scélérat; guerre / paix; fraternité / haine; vie / mort; charmant / affreux; bonheur / malheur.* The pole actually signified is not that of the pastoral *foyer*, but that of historical destruction, yet Tellmarch's discovery of his guilt is perhaps less devastating than his confrontation with radical interpretive doubt. When history is the signifying matrix, good deeds are bad deeds, human beings are not human, and a single sign can mean both life and death.

Between his departure from Tellmarch and his setting of the fire which gave off this polyvalent smoke, Lantenac has a similar encounter with the indeterminacy of meaning. While attempting to locate Royalist forces, he is suddenly surrounded by a huge band of armed men carrying a tricolor flag. Certain that he is about to die, the marquis defiantly identifies himself to see his captors become his subjects; the army is White, the tricolor flag a captured trophy. Where Tellmarch is powerless to interpret, Lantenac is powerless to represent, and the text glosses his impotence in this way:

> La légende raconte qu'il y avait dans les vieilles forêts thuringiennes des êtres étranges, race des géants, plus et moins qu'hommes, qui étaient considérés par les Romains comme des animaux horribles et par les Germains comme des incarnations divines, et qui, selon la rencontre, couraient la chance d'être exterminés ou adorés.
>
> Le marquis éprouva quelque chose de pareil à ce que devait ressentir un de ces êtres quand, s'attendant à être traité comme un monstre, il était brusquement traité comme un dieu. (p. 109)

That Lantenac's experience of historical meaning provokes a tale of legendary hermeneutics is not surprising in a novel which asserts that "l'histoire et la légende ont le même but, peindre sous l'homme momentané l'homme éternel" (p. 220). Yet the novel also shows that there is an insuperable obstacle to either history or legend achieving its goal. There is no way to go "under" momentary existence to discover eternal essence. Are the Germanic giants gods or monsters? It is impossible to answer, for their definition derives uniquely from the interpretive stance assumed by those they encounter. Indeterminate until a social community assigns them a sense, they are as incapable of defining themselves as Lantenac, who is a liberator or a traitor according to the historical vision of those who understand him. The text which declares that the eternal underlies the momentary develops a multitude of ways to show characters' inability to preserve anything meaningful beneath the transitory significance created by a revolutionary process. What history paints under momentary meaning is momentary meaning.

Even when the speaker is Gauvain. The momentous effect of historical situation is in fact particularly apparent in the novel's failure to insulate Gauvain from situational redefinition, a failure all the more striking because of the several devices which attempt to set Gauvain apart. Although incontestably its hero, Gauvain appears in less than a quarter of the novel's five hundred pages, an implicit admission of how difficult it is to depict unambiguously correct behavior in representation of historical events. Moreover, Gauvain's commitment to the Revolution's goals does not require that he do the dirty work necessary to implement them. In the novel's political allegory, he embodies only half of the Revolution, the good half. The bad half is Cimourdain, a severance which eliminates ambivalence by keeping good and evil, life and death, as properly apart in the world as in semantic structure.

> Ces deux hommes incarnaient, l'un la mort, l'autre la vie. . . . C'était comme une âme coupée en deux, et partagée; Gauvain, en effet, avait reçu une moitié de l'âme de Cimourdain, mais la moitié douce. Il semblait que Gauvain avait eu le rayon blanc et que Cimourdain avait gardé pour lui ce qu'on pourrait appeler le rayon noir. (pp. 283-84)

The Revolution teaches characters like Tellmarch that meaning is the effect of a code and that codes vary with historical conditions. Gauvain recognizes only one language for humanity, and in it signs are as immutably beautiful as they are unwaveringly true. "Amnistie est pour moi le plus beau mot de *la langue humaine*" (p. 289).

Present in less than a quarter of the novel, Gauvain is further protected by the fact that more than half the pages that do describe him narrate his ascent above royalty and revolution. To judge from the few historically grounded passages in which he appears, this was a wise strategy. Despite his sterling qualities—maybe especially because of his sterling qualities—Gauvain wavers like any other sense-bearing unit when he is incorporated into historical discourse, as he is in the chapter entitled "Les Deux Pôles du vrai" which reports his conversation with Cimourdain. That title itself suggests a shift away from static certainty, for the truth which is a child (p. 433) and is above revolutions (p. 208) has only one pole. Gauvain is no better equipped for bipolarity than Tellmarch; for example, he acts only on the basis of a rigid code of martial honor: "Je ne fais pas la guerre aux femmes. . . . Je ne fais pas la guerre aux vieillards. . . . Je ne fais pas la guerre aux enfants" (pp. 284-85). Cimourdain's response is a crushing instance of historical reference as refutation of eternal principles: "sache qu'il faut faire la guerre à la femme quand elle se nomme Marie Antoinette, au vieillard quand il se nomme Pie VI, pape, et à l'enfant quand il se nomme Louis Capet" (p. 285). Cimourdain's triple "naming" transformation is a properly referential version of the statement made by the political content assigned common nouns throughout the novel. To name a thing by a historical label is to necessitate historical interpretation, which does not function on the basis of stable definitions.

A conscious revolutionary recognizes this but looks forward to the day when historical decoding will be unnecessary:

> La révolution extirpe la royauté dans le roi, l'aristocratie dans le noble, le despotisme dans le soldat, la superstitition dans le prêtre, la barbarie dans le juge, en un mot, tout ce qui est la tyrannie dans tout ce qui est le tyran. (p. 287)

Such extirpation of vices is also an extirpation of semes, precisely the elimination of historical sense necessary to reveal the human core of words like *roi, noble, soldat, prêtre, juge.* One would expect this to be Gauvain's goal, yet it is Cimourdain, the man who recognizes that only violence can alter the signifying systems by which societies understand themselves, who states the admirable purpose of converting kings into men.

Gauvain even effects the opposite transformation, defending his constant release of prisoners by repeating that he cannot kill a "man" except under honorable conditions. Those he did not kill have become vicious leaders of reactionary bands, however; instead of depoliticizing them, Gauvain regularly converts harmless prisoners into political weapons. As Cimourdain informs him, "En sauvant ces deux *hommes,* tu as donné deux *ennemis à la République*" (p. 285). The lameness of Gauvain's rejoinder manifests the impossibility of preserving eternal codes in the French Revolution: "Certes, je voudrais lui faire des amis, et non lui donner des ennemis" (pp. 285-86). The conditional tense is suited to Gauvain's conditional value—to his own humane ideals as well as to the Revolution.

Cimourdain first arrives in the Vendée just in time to save Gauvain's life by taking onto himself a saber thrust meant for his spiritual son. The wound makes Cimourdain's face a "red mask" which prevents Gauvain from recognizing the preserver who lies before him wearing the clothes of a political delegate. A surgeon removes the insignia and washes away the blood, thus revealing a man beneath the envoy and a face behind the mask. Meanwhile, Gauvain finds Cimourdain's name among his papers and is transported by joy: " 'Comité de salut public. Le citoyen Cimourdain. . . . Cimourdain! Mon maître!' 'Ton père,' dit Cimourdain" (p. 271).

That sequence is a striking example of the play with codes and messages in *Quatrevingt-Treize.* Cimourdain first appears to Gauvain as a tricolor sash, political papers from the Committee of Public Safety, and blood spilled in a battle. Revelation of the delegate's physical humanity coincides with Gauvain's emotional identification, which in turn provokes the *citoyen* to give himself the radiantly human name of *père.* The father's next utterance, however, is in a different code, one with a decidedly situational base. Gauvain pardons an enemy soldier and thus brings his tutor to mutter, "En effet, c'est un clément" (p. 274). In that utterance, *clément* is used in the pejorative sense assigned it by the historical language used by Marat, Danton, and Robespierre, and Cimourdain the father again becomes Cimourdain the political delegate, unable to speak to his son.

Gauvain and Cimourdain's reunion thus pointedly raises the difficulty of how historical and eternal speakers are to communicate with one another. However, rather than confront that problem, the central dilemma of the novel, the text leaves it in suspension and seeks a way out. It finds it by brusquely transferring its attention to Michelle Fléchard, whose uniquely maternal character is incomparably less ambivalent than Cimourdain's paternity. Michelle again functions as an escape hatch after Cimourdain and Gauvain's discussion of historical meaning, which ends with Cimourdain redefining *pitié* as he had earlier redefined *clément*; pity can be one of the forms of treason (p. 289), he says, and Gauvain does not reply. As if to preclude the possibility of its hero's silence implying the validity of Cimourdain's understanding, the text immediately reverts to its most pitiable figure, the mother without her babies. The transition is the chapter title "Dolorosa," whose allusion to the non-French and nonhistorical *mater dolorosa* assertively proclaims that the codes of the French Revolution are no longer pertinent. The first sentence of "Dolorosa" is "Cependant la mère cherchait ses petits"— meanwhile and nevertheless, the mother was seeking her little ones. The novel which ends by leaving history for dawn and flowers intermittently prefigures its conclusion by sudden withdrawals to that other leg of the pastoral torso, a mother and her children.

This chapter began with the question of whether a good deed can be a bad deed. The fact that within history the answer is yes leads *Quatrevingt-Treize* to affirm a representational system in which the answer is no. Gauvain's good deed, the salvation of Lantenac, is identical to that of Tellmarch. The second rescue is divine and the first infernal because *Quatrevingt-Treize* assumes in the interim a moral perspective to which practical consequences are irrelevant. When the novel decides that mankind "breaks, shatters, sterilizes, and kills" meanings as well as worlds, it responds by exalting a purely verbal form of signification within which good is good and pity is pity as surely as the sun rises and the lily remains itself. With the stars hidden by revolutionary clouds, Gauvain rises above the storm to gaze at a light which human beings in time and space cannot see.

6

The Impotence of Speech

Certainly the best-known, and arguably the best-written, passage in *Quatrevingt-Treize* is the stunning anthology piece which describes a wheeled ship's cannon broken loose from its mooring. The rolling sea makes the cannon into a horrible weapon, seemingly systematic in its devastation of ship and sailors. The stylistic *tour de force* by which Hugo conveys the unimaginable fury of an inanimate object has many features which reward study, but for our purposes its major interest is its use of extraordinary language to contest the set vision of the world that ordinary language encodes. When an event violently challenges our representation of what can occur, the semiotic system through which we represent is invalidated. "Dire l'épouvante est impossible" (p. 41) because the language by which we say what we know is impotent if we are constrained to say what we do not know.

The cannon becomes the inconceivable, a material cause without a formal cause, "l'entrée en liberté de la matière" (p. 39). The oppositions by which we divide the world into segmented categories are not pertinent to a situation in which blindness seems to have eyes (p. 45) and what is dead is at the same time alive (p. 39). When the cannon leaves the corpus of "*ce que nous appelons les objets inertes*" (p. 39), the linguistic system which permits us to call things by any name loses its credibility, as is most apparent when the text abandons the combinatorial restrictions of [+animate] and [−animate] terms.

The animateness feature is basic to a huge number of selection restrictions on which action can go with which agent, which modifier with which substantive. We cannot normally speak of an "irritated floor" or say that "the wrench changed its mind." But when [+animate] and [−animate] words are equated— the cannon becomes a beast (p. 38), the machine a monster (p. 38)—all selection restrictions expressing a difference between what is alive and what is inert are rejected.

Cette masse court . . . va, vient, s'arrête, paraît méditer, reprend sa course, traverse comme une flèche le navire d'un bout à l'autre, pirouette, se dérobe, s'évade, se cabre, heurte, ébrèche, tue, extermine. . . . la colère de l'inanimé. . . . bloc forcené. . . . brute de bronze. . . . un projectile qui se ravise. . . . un plan incliné qui a des caprices. . . . de la ruse dans cette masse. . . . le canon avait l'air de comprendre. (pp. 38-46)

The whole of the representational system called French is made to appear inadequate when the Latin title "Vis et vir" introduces the chapter on the damage done by a chain attached to the cannon's *vis*, the breech "screw" used to adjust its aim. In French, *vis* implies inertness, in Latin it states power, and the latter sense is incomparably more appropriate to a *vis* which holds its chain in a grip of steel and wields it like a weapon (p. 46).

Since Hugo's success in depicting a runaway cannon clearly depends in no way on his ability to evoke experiential knowledge stored in his readers' mental encyclopedias, it may seem strange to be discussing this passage in a study whose major theoretical argument is that the referential fallacy is not fallacious. Description of the agony of the corvette *Claymore* works magnificently because it exploits the resources offered by language alone. The combinatorial restrictions of inanimate words are a verbal, not a referential, fact. Nevertheless, this apparent exercise in *écriture* is organically connected to the novel's vision of referential signification, for it too displays the invasion of verbal structure by (fictitious) extraverbal events. An experience made the neat ordering of the animate/inanimate opposition appear ludicrous, just as the French Revolution made the neat order of the Old Regime's language an archaic residue. Like the language of history, the language of the avenging cannon makes A ≠ A and posits the nonverbal world as the reason. When either political or physical tumult explodes concepts of reality, the language encoding those concepts is ripped apart as well.

There is another link between the Revolution and the shrewd iron on the *Claymore*, one whose hackneyed ancestry does not prevent *Quatrevingt-Treize* from employing it to great effect. The shifting support furnished the cannon by the sea is analogous to that given the ship of state by historical change. "Etre un membre de la Convention, c'était être une vague de l'Ocean. . . . [la Révolution] emportait celui-ci en écume et brisait celui-là aux écueils" (p. 207). Under revolutionary leaders are forces identical to those under the runaway cannon, movements whose strength and menace are in their cumulative and reciprocal effects.

[Le canon] est remué par le navire, qui est remué par la mer, qui est remué par le vent.(p. 39)

Ceci est une loi. Mirabeau sent remuer à une profondeur inconnue Robespierre, Robespierre sent remuer Marat, Marat sent remuer Hébert, Hébert sent remuer Babœuf. (p. 168)

The historically referential language of proper names like Marat, Robespierre, Hébert, and Babœuf conveys a sense that repudiates the conventions of ordinary discourse. Accordingly, serial inclusion of those names assumes the vocabulary and imagery previously used to illustrate the irrelevance of ordinary discourse to description of a ship's destruction by one of its own cannon.

The three parts of *Quatrevingt-Treize* are entitled "En Mer," "A Paris," and "En Vendée"; all three situate narrative in a treacherously shifting environment. The referential "Paris" and "Vendée" connote the same peril as the sea; Tellmarch is as unable to keep his good deed a good deed as the *Claymore* is to reach its chosen port. Whether their subject is the course of a revolution or the motion of a sea, violations of standard linguistic conventions in *Quatrevingt-Treize* express a single theme: revelation of an unforeseen world requires an unforeseen code for its communication.

But the novel's thrust toward pastoral meaning battles against precisely such unforeseen codes, and the defusing of historical language has an intriguing corollary in the absolution of maritime language. During the text's most extensive representation of the pastoral universe, depiction of the captured Fléchard children at one with a natural world where "tout aimait tout" (p. 346), part of the colossal sweetness is the tale of little Georgette's trip to rejoin her brothers. As the grating noise of historical conflct enters the children's world only as musical harmonies (pp. 332, 336), so the language of the sea appears in description of their world not as a structureless and disturbing figure of the unknown but as the charming imagery of an infant's contemplation of a universe too big for it. Georgette is separated from her brothers by the paraphernalia littering a library-turned-storeroom, and the narrative of her journey to rejoin them adapts the vocabulary of "En Mer" to radically different effect:

> [L]e trajet était hérissé de difficultés . . . tout un archipel d'écueils. Georgette s'y hasarda. Elle . . . s'engagea dans les récifs, serpenta dans les détroits . . . et parvint ainsi à ce qu'un marin appellerait la mer libre . . . [une échelle] faisait entre Georgette et ses frères une sorte de cap à franchir . . . elle se redressa, doubla le promontoire, regarda René-Jean et Gros-Alain, et rit. (pp. 333-34)

Maritime language was earlier another of the forms the novel employed to say something new. In description of Georgette, it acquires a subject as ancient as the mother love to which the prologue assigns the language of a newly declared republic. The effect is in both cases the same: the discourse of a situationally created sense metamorphoses into the sense of a discursively delimited creation.

Book III of Part III of *Quatrevingt-Treize*, which describes the Fléchard children at play, is a kind of sterile zone against the infection of mutable meaning. Gauvain must struggle against men who represent the world historically in order to preserve the pastoral simplicity of the "langue humaine" in which amnesty is a universal and eternal value. Without struggle, the Fléchard children appear as those "que *toutes les langues humaines* appellent les faibles et les bénis" (p. 347). Semiotic conventions which can be refuted by external events are forgotten during depiction of three childish allegories, incarnations of that which is respected by all peoples for all time and is so designated in all representational systems. When Lantenac responds to the scream of Michelle Fléchard, "cette mère [qui] était la maternité" (p. 414), when Gauvain accepts the imperative of the "protection due aux faibles par les forts" (p. 442), they are agonistically asserting the vision of the world which children effortlessly experience as absorption into cosmic harmony. "[I]l y avait de la maternité dans l'infini; . . . il semblait que l'on sentît quelqu'un d'invisible prendre ces mystérieuses précautions qui dans le redoutable conflit des êtres protègent les chétifs contre les forts" (pp. 346-47).

Although the epitome of pastoral discourse, Book III of Part III has a resoundingly historical title, "Le Massacre de Saint-Barthélemy." Referentially, that title designates the slaughter of French Protestants ordered by Catherine de Médicis. Textually, it designates three children who rip apart an antique quarto volume purported to be the gospel according to Saint Bartholomew. The novel thus extracts the name of one of the most momentous events in French history from the corpus of referential terms and makes it label the innocence of play, a semiotic exculpation repeated in the brutal vocabulary stating the children's delight in their game. "Il en est de la première page arrachée comme du premier sang versé. Cela décide le carnage" (p. 342). "L'appétit de la destruction existe" (p. 344); "Ce fut une extermination" (p. 345). After removing all the pages from the book, the children shred them and throw the pieces into the air, fascinated by the butterfly-like movements they produce; "Et le massacre se termina par un évanouissement dans l'azur" (p. 346). That sentence, which ends the tale of the book's extermination, is untranslatable because it does two things at once. While describing the fluttering paper of a children's game, it perfectly summarizes Gauvain's apotheosis. The Republican general also ends massacres by an *évanouissement dans l'azur*, the ascent of his soul into the sun-soaked domain where historical sense is as unintelligible as in Georgette's playroom.

The presence of a book entitled "Le Massacre de Saint-Barthélemy" in a novel entitled *Quatrevingt-Treize* recalls lines from "Ecrit en 1846," the poem in which Hugo defends his liberalism against the accusation that he treacherously renounced his monarchist past.

> J'ai lu, j'ai comparé l'aube avec la nuit noire,
> Et les quatrevingt-treize aux Saint-Barthélemy.

In those lines, the Saint Bartholomew's massacre is to the Old Regime what '93 is to the new, blood spilled and suffering inflicted for the sake of a political system. But where "Ecrit en 1846" chooses the new system over the old because execution to safeguard the dawn is preferable to slaughter for the black night, *Quatrevingt-Treize* consigns both to oblivion. *Saint-Barthélemy* and *quatrevingt-treize* are equally historical, signs whose meaning derives from human events. The text forcibly inserts them into a representational system hermetically cut off from human events. In the final chapter, the castle and the guillotine are opposed so as to plead the necessity of a third option, supplied by the sight of the rising sun and the smell of blooming blossoms. The bloody dates of France's monarchist and republican periods are analogously dissolved, this time in the smiling faces of three children who do not know what either means.

This ignorance of history has its corollary in the Fléchard children's familiarity with nature.

> Le ciel était bleu, il faisait chaud, il faisait beau. La frêle créature, sans rien savoir, sans rien connaître, sans rien comprendre, mollement noyée dans la rêverie qui ne pense pas, se sentait en sureté dans cette nature, dans ces arbres honnêtes, dans cette verdure sincère, dans cette campagne pure et paisible, dans ces bruits de nids, de sources, de mouches, de feuilles, au-dessus desquels resplendissait l'immense innocence du soleil. (p. 330)

That passage predicts the novel's final equation of its antihistorical stance with condemnation of human existence itself. Georgette, the "frail creature," assumes the textual form of a quadruple denial of normal mental competence—*sans rien savoir, sans rien connaître, sans rien comprendre, qui ne pense pas.* The human modifiers "sincere" and "honest" describe trees and their leaves, not men and their words, and the noises that matter are the twittering of tiny birds rather than articulated speech. Mankind's capacity to create meaning by the bloody actions which gave their sense to *Saint-Barthélemy* and *quatrevingt-treize* vitiates human representation in its entirety. Since what humans say and understand is too often befouled by what they do, the words which encode human meaning are perpetually suspect beside the immense innocence of a sun and a little girl.

The Fléchard children emit a "bégaiement," a "chuchotement," a "gazouillement," but not a *parole*, not human speech. What they mean is not expressible in the semiotic system able to state what adults do, so their sounds are of necessity another order of signification.

> Le murmure de l'enfant, c'est plus et moins que la parole; ce ne sont pas des notes, et c'est un chant; ce ne sont pas des syllabes, et c'est un langage; ce murmure a eu son commencement dans le ciel et n'aura pas sa fin sur la terre; il est d'avant la naissance, et il continue, c'est une suite. (p. 329)

One of Saussure's fundamental distinctions was between *langue* and *parole*—language and speech—the former a social institution, the latter its individual execution. The Fléchard children, expressing neither through a socially defined *langue* nor an individually generated *parole*, create words that are instead a transcendent *langage*, a human potential without connections to the separate *langues* that realize it in societies. Both eternal and universal, a child's murmur begins in heaven and does not end on earth. Ordinary human speech is subject to signifying wrongly by grounding sense in concrete situations. Children's murmur runs no such risk, for it communicates with the sun about heaven rather than with human agents about human action.

"Le Massacre de Saint-Barthélemy" is unique among the fourteen books of *Quatrevingt-Treize* because it alone does not assign titles to its chapters. This silence is another suggestion that the failures of historical signification condemn human semiosis as a whole. In moving toward its goal of globally refuting the meaning articulated by signs like *Saint-Barthélemy*, the novel prefers blank spaces to words. Dehistoricization of meaning is accomplished by dissolving the name of a political massacre into a pastoral expression of "on ne sait quel appel inconscient à la justice éternelle" (p. 329). The signifying forms suited to labeling historical narratives, conscious appeals to justice in time, are inappropriate to such a project. The sterile zone against historical signs must in the extreme include all other human signs as well as its "évanouissement dans l'azur."

Such denigration of historical discourse in Part III directly contradicts the power accorded it in those portions of Part I which follow the prologue, a power poetically announced in an early chapter title, "La Parole, c'est Le Verbe"—speech is the Logos, mankind's words have the material effects of the Godhead's. That title is given to a passage in which Lantenac delivers an eloquent political harangue that converts a man determined to kill him into a creature selflessly devoted to him and his cause. Unconsciously confirming the chapter title, the would-be murderer begs forgiveness by telling Lantenac, "Vous parlez comme le bon Dieu" (p. 73).

Yet the Good Lord's speech, annihilating the value assigned familial words in pastoral discourse, forces "enfant" and "fils" into ideological rhetoric within which history alone confers semantic weight: "Dieu souffre dans son fils très-chrétien le roi de France qui est enfant comme l'enfant Jésus et qui est en prison dans la tour du Temple" (p. 71). The sailor who wanted to kill Lantenac is the brother of a man whom Lantenac had executed. The murder was thus projected in the name of a familial code, precisely the code made nonpertinent when Lantenac's oration incorporates "mère" as the object of "tuer" and "frère" and "fils" as objects of "fusiller." The speech that is the Logos is speech which gleefully subordinates familial meaning to historical conditions.

In its superbly ordered defense of the Old Regime, Lantenac's harangue to the man bent on murdering him prefigures his speech to the nephew bent on rescuing him. The first ideological outburst demonstrates that speech is the Logos, the second leads to revelation that the Logos is impervious to speech.

Because Gauvain has entered a realm where historical conditons are unalterably subordinate to familial meanings, his response to Lantenac's rhetoric is silent meditation. The Word has changed its nature in a transformation paralleling that effected by a second identification of Lantenac with God, one which occurs after the Fléchard children's rescue inaugurates the final validation of pastoral meaning. Sergeant Radoub's joy at rediscovering his adopted family makes him shout the formula which first expressed parental affection in the prologue, *Vive la République.* Lantenac responds with *Vive le roi,* thus prompting Radoub to comment, "Tu peux bien crier tout ce que tu voudras et dire des bêtises si tu veux, tu es le bon Dieu" (p. 424). The first character to call Lantenac the Good Lord does so because his vision of the world has just been politicized, the second becaus. the world he sees has just been depoliticized. Only in historical discourse are Radoub's *Vive la République* and Lantenac's *Vive le roi* antonymous. In the language used to describe devotion to children, they have identical senses.

When *roi* and *République* do appear in the discourse which defines them as opposites, the result is cacophony. In Book I, the corvette *Claymore*'s encounter with the French fleet begins in this way:

> Et un coup de canon partit de la corvette.
> —Vive le roi! cria l'équipage.
> Alors on entendit au fond de l'horizon un autre cri, immense, lointain, confus, distinct pourtant:
> —Vive la République!
> Et un bruit pareil au bruit de trois cents foudres éclata dans les profondeurs de l'océan. (p. 65)

The ear-splitting noise of three hundred thunderbolts is a distinguishing trait of historical speech throughout *Quatrevingt-Treize.* Marat, Robespierre, and Danton communicate only in "éclats de parole" (p. 148). The members of the Convention, who share the power to turn words into reality, are further like Lantenac in making both words and reality inhumanly horrible.

> Il s'est dit à cette tribune de ces vertigineuses paroles qui ont, quelquefois à l'insu même de celui qui les prononce, l'accent fatidique des révolutions, et à la suite desquels les faits matériels paraissent avoir brusquement on ne sait quoi de mécontent et de passionné . . . les catastrophes surviennent furieuses et comme exaspérées par les paroles des hommes. (pp. 204-05)

"L'accent fatidique des révolutions" identifies that form of discourse in which history's tangible presence makes words give life and life give meaning, in which verbal structure and "material facts" are a continuum. When meaning is a matter of situation, catastrophes occur without foreknowledge or intention. As a consequence, the communicative circuit goes from horror to horror instead of from person to person, and words whose sense ought to transcend situations appear only in negated constructions stating the absence of their referents.

> Pas de grâce! (mot d'ordre de la Commune). —Pas de quartier! (mot d'ordre des princes). (p. 114)

> Pas de grâce! pas de prisonniers! était le cri des deux partis. L'histoire était pleine d'une ombre terrible. (p. 308)

> La terreur répliquait à la terreur. (p. 223)

Because historically degraded speech elicits a historically degraded rejoinder, "La terreur répliquait à la terreur" is one of many sentences in *Quatrevingt-Treize* that use a word associated with verbal contact to express an exchange of nonverbal savagery; for example, "Le tonnerre assaillant répliqua au tonnerre embusqué. Les détonations se ripostèrent" (p. 381). Use of such a lexicon to denote slaughter rather than communication is natural in *Quatrevingt-Treize*, where historical speech is not itself communication in the sense of an exchange of pastorally stable signs. The "répliques" and "ripostes" of Danton, Marat, and Robespierre are no different from those of armies in mortal combat: "Ils continuèrent sur un ton de causerie dont la lenteur accentuait la violence des répliques et des ripostes" (pp. 161-62). The irony of "ton de causerie" further denigrates historical speech as the form of communication in which violence rather than meaning is conveyed from person to person.

Hence the necessity for Gauvain to develop a different order of response during his transfiguration.

> Gauvain était chargé de lui donner [à Lantenac] la réplique.
> La lutte des passions bonnes et des passions mauvaises faisaient en ce moment sur le monde le chaos; Lantenac, dominant ce chaos, venait d'en dégager l'humanité; c'était à Gauvain maintenant d'en dégager la famille. (p. 443)

The reborn Gauvain does not communicate with Lantenac, he communes with him. The response he gives is above the domain of historically chaotic meaning because it is above the domain of speech itself. The mystical silence enveloping Gauvain as he awaits death condemns the inferior signification effected by ordinary language, which earlier defined even Gauvain's *parole* situationally.

> —Lantenac est l'ennemi de la patrie. Le duel entre lui et moi ne peut finir que par sa mort, ou la mienne.
> —Gauvain, souviens-toi de cette parole.
> —Elle est dite. (p. 286)

Mankind's mutable *parole*, which admits exceptions to mercy no matter whose mouth speaks of it, defines signs contextually. Gauvain's renunciation of the

Republic is therefore of necessity a renunciation of speech as well. The rest is silence.

If there is a good deal of silliness in the novel's cloying insistence on the moral triumph radiating from Gauvain's silent renunciation, there is also a good deal of honesty in the separation of such purity from human acts and words in space and time. The same mixture of idealist moral vision and concrete historical reference is apparent in the novel's uncomfortable effort to isolate good from evil in the Revolution as a whole. The text at times assumes an Olympian perspective permitting it to make nonsensical calculations like the precise proportion of "human" and "political" motives behind the Convention's 11,210 decrees (p. 203). In an extraction comparable to Lantenac and Gauvain's domination of chaos to preserve humanity and the family, the Revolution is given a timeless component unpolluted by its occurrence in history. "De ce chaos d'ombre et de cette tumultueuse fuite de nuages, sortaient d'immenses rayons de lumière parallèles aux lois éternelles" (p. 202). Some men, in the Revolution without being of it, are in fact immune to historical meaning. "Parmi ces éloquences furieuses, parmi ces voix hurlantes et grondantes, il y avait des silences féconds; Lakanal se taisait, et combinait dans sa pensée l'éducation publique nationale; [etc.]" (p. 196).

The glory of *Quatrevingt-Treize* is that such saccharine statements appear as alien to the world the novel represents as Balzac's monarchism appears to the world of the *Comédie humaine*. Parallel rays and eternal laws do not survive exposure to the dialectical conflicts and historical meanings palpable in the novel's depiction of a revolution which transmutes humanity into classes and good into evil. Although Gauvain's final silence is in theory as "fecund" as Lakanal's, it stands as dreamy rumination on Utopian twaddle within the context the text supplies for it. Parallel beams do not emerge from chaos for the same reason that eternal meanings do not organize the sense making of historical agents, because the foundation determines the superstructure erected on it. The text's presentation of historical situations continually undermines its impulse toward transhistorical truth, a contradiction culminating in the absolute dichotomy between divine beauty and social ugliness in the last chapter. The failure of the text's attempt to present history as an inconsequential setting for humanity's progress toward immemorial goals testifies to the intensity with which the text also presents the fact that history is awesomely consequential.

In the prologue, the mother expresses sempiternal feelings in language impervious to situational interpretation. As the text develops, that language appears less and less adequate to the communication required by the experience of revolution. When history separates Michelle Fléchard from her children, language loses its ability to make existence comprehensible. The mother consequently uses it to state its own inadequacy, then abandons it definitively. " 'Sans mes enfants, est-ce que je suis? Je voudrais que quelqu'un m'expliquât pourquoi je n'ai pas mes enfants. Je sens bien qu'il se passe quelque chose, puisque je ne comprends pas.' . . . A partir de ce jour, elle ne parla plus" (p. 279). Tellmarch, Michelle's doctor, acquiesces in his patient's rejection of human meaning as distorted by historical events. "Il se taisait de son côté, comprenant, devant un tel accablement, l'impuissance de la parole" (p. 280).

Speech's impotence condemns the species identified by speech, and Michelle imitates Tellmarch in listening to the birds instead of to men. In doing so, she regresses to the instinctual level of subsemiotic behavior.

> La maternité est sans issue; on ne discute pas avec elle. Ce qui fait qu'une mère est sublime, c'est que c'est une espèce de bête. L'instinct maternel est divinement animal. La mère n'est plus femme, elle est femelle. (p. 280)

"Divinement animal" perfectly summarizes what Michelle becomes, an amalgam of beings above and below humanity but not a human. She represents the same bridge across mankind's place in the chain of beings when her shriek extracts first Lantenac and then Gauvain from history.

> Ce cri de l'inexprimable angoisse n'est donné qu'aux mères. Rien n'est plus farouche et rien n'est plus touchant. Quand une femme le jette, on croit entendre une louve; quand une louve le pousse, on croit entendre une femme. . . . Cette mère, c'était la maternité; tout ce qui résume l'humanité est surhumain . . . elle avait le cri de la bête et le geste de la déesse. (pp. 413-14)

The beast's scream and the goddess's gesture are alike in one thing: they do not signify through the conventions of human semiosis. It is those conventions as a whole that the text ultimately rejects, replacing them with the nonverbal communion between Michelle and Lantenac, Lantenac and Gauvain.

The contradiction between the text's validation of stable signs with stable meanings and its representation of a revolution that questions all signs and all meanings is the novel's fundamental tension. At one and the same time, human sense is impotent and omnipotent, inadequate to what matters in life and adequate to the overthrow of what makes life matter. The impotence of speech which Tellmarch feels as he watches a grieving mother is also evident in the blank spaces heading the chapters on the Fléchard children in God's hands and in Gauvain's silent contemplation of the world God will make, for transhistorical visions cannot be represented in the discourse which emerges from the creative action of historical agents. A series of variants repeat the novel's development from its first to its last sentence, from historical reference to a string of words announcing their purely verbal status. *Quatrevingt-Treize* is a masterpiece because it demonstrates that each of these developments leads away from representational systems adequate to human experience in history.

Those Parisians Storming Heaven

The standard criticism to which authors leave themselves open when, like Hugo, they set out to "disengage the Revolution from horror," is that they end up disengaging the Revolution from the Revolution and willy-nilly validate Burke's position that the Old Regime could have evolved so as to deal with France's problems in a wiser, calmer, and more successful way than the groups which actually seized state power. Still compelling are R. R. Palmer's comments against those who accept the Revolution's goals and deplore its methods.

> So long as one thinks it to have been wise, feasible or legitimate to try to introduce a kind of political democracy in France in the eighteenth century, one must regard as necessary . . . virtually all the steps taken by the revolutionaries down to the dictatorship of 1793-4. To consider these steps unnecessary, deploring them as "excesses," requires one to say that the objective of political democracy at the time was a false or impossible one, which should have been given up as the means necessary to attain it became apparent.[1]

As Mao said, a revolution is not the same thing as an afternoon tea. To will a change in social structure is to will the violence required to accomplish it.

Among the most remarkable aspects of *Quatrevingt-Treize* is that, as a complete text, it cannot be condemned for attempting to separate revolutionary goats from revolutionary sheep so as to keep only the good half. Rather than disengaging the Revolution from horror, it disengages its characters from the Revolution. Within history, Tellmarch and Gauvain are not pure. It is only by a mystical ascent above royalty and revolution that their narratives attain the Good and the Beautiful. The novel presents Marat, Danton, and Robespierre as the hellish voices of violent rage but not as self-serving perverters of the forces supporting them. Despite its ghastly concentration on blood and fire, the dialogue between the Tourgue and the guillotine appears as an inevitable confrontation. Striving to present humanity as immutably directed toward timeless goals while also presenting it within the matrix of historically determined processes, the text must eventually choose between immutability and humanity. The fact that its choice rejects human activity and human speech is far less objectionable than would have been a tortuously convoluted assertion that mankind is impervious to its historical situation. The antihistorical stance of *Quatrevingt-Treize* developed from recognition that, because history is conflict and contradiction, a vision of the world which excludes conflict must also exclude history. In the absolute opposition between pastoral and historical representation, the former is as inadequate to the French Revolution as the latter is to a baby girl's pink toes.

Quatrevingt-Treize was written under the shock of the tumultuous events of Hugo's *année terrible*, the time of the Franco-Prussian war and the Paris Commune of 1871. Those same events provoked Hippolyte Taine's shift to historical research, and the comprehensive lucidity of *Quatrevingt-Treize* can best be appreciated by comparing the novel to the vitriolic assaults on revolutionary leaders and political instability in Taine's *Origines de la France contemporaine*. Almost unique among French men of letters, Victor Hugo was led by the experience of the Commune not to a denial or falsification of the historical process but to luminous presentation of history as human agents creating their world. The eventual refusal of that form of creation in *Quatrevingt-Treize* is inseparable from profound awareness that social events constrain human beings to adapt in ways incomprehensible apart from the specific situations in which they developed.

Quatrevingt-Treize thus couples acute historical consciousness with passionate refusal of its implications, a paradoxical combination whose origin is in Hugo's personal experience of history during the period which preceded and provoked the novel's composition. The terrible year transformed a decades-old plan for a book on the Revolution into a text begun and completed in less than six months. Examination of history in the text leads to consideration of the text in history, in the series of events which converted the revolutionary tradition inherited from 1793 into the concept of revolution which has made our century what it is. Both its extraordinary sensitivity to historical meaning and its puerile insistence on pastoral escape are intimately related to the fact that *Quatrevingt-Treize* grew out of the Paris Commune and its aftermath.

After a nineteen-year exile in unwavering opposition to Napoleon III, Hugo experienced violently contradictory emotions at the outbreak of the Franco-Prussian war in July of 1870. A French victory would mean a more solid regime and the probability of exile until death; the end of exile, on the other hand, would almost certainly result only from a French defeat, unthinkable to the son of General Hugo who believed with all his heart and mind in the glorious allegiance and valor of France's soldiers. When Hugo left Guernsey for Brussels to await the course of events, his plans were completely unsettled. He was prepared for anything, even for assuming despotic powers over his countrymen. The meditations in his notebooks on what his behavior as a dictator should be are an extraordinary instance of a genius's stupidity.

Dictatorship. I shall bear the burden of it. If I fail, I will punish myself by eternal exile.

If I succeed, dictatorship is a crime. The success of a crime does not absolve it. I will have committed that crime. I will do justice to myself and, even if I have saved the Republic, I declare that I will leave France never to return.

Successful or unsuccessful, I shall punish myself for dictatorship by eternal exile.

Here are the conditions:

dictatorship without limit

dictatorship without defense.[2]

Such egregious nonsense is fortunately limited to the journal entries from Hugo's brief stay in Brussels. When he finally entered France on September 5, 1870, the crushing Prussian victory at Sedan had already led to proclamation of the Republic and formation of a new government in which he was not included. Despite the throngs who greeted his return with such enthusiasm that they "compensated (him) in an hour for twenty years of exile,"[3] despite his fully justified doubts concerning the capacities and commitment of the new leaders, Hugo insisted that he had "not come to topple the provisional government of the Republic but to support it."[4] Although he may secretly have hoped that France would eventually replace those who had sworn allegiance to the hated Empire with the incorruptible exile who had never compromised his republican integrity, Hugo did in fact support the provisional regime throughout his stay in Paris. His name was prominent among those proposed for a new government during the uprisings of October 31, 1870, and January 22, 1871. On both occasions, Hugo rebuked the insurgents and urged support for the men who, albeit with monstrous ineptitude, were conducting the struggle against Prussia.

As his part in that struggle, Hugo had, immediately after his return to Paris, the astounding idea of issuing a call "To the Germans," summoning them to put down their arms for the love of French and Parisian contributions to civilization. Bismarck did not respond. Ten days after Hugo's appeal, Paris was besieged. The poet also issued calls "To the French" and "To the Parisians," both exhorting greater efforts from regular and irregular forces. The rhetoric of the three calls was uniformly vigorous, their effect uniformly nil. French armies went from defeat to ignominy, Paris was bombarded, and, on January 28, 1871, an armistice was signed as the first step toward surrendering Alsace and Lorraine to the Prussians.

Between his return to Paris and the armistice, Hugo amply demonstrated the prodigious complexity of his personality. With admirable self-sacrifice, he abandoned all author's rights for the many public readings of Les Châtiments, now a legal instead of an underground best-seller. With ludicrous vanity, he strolled through Paris to inspire its citizens with words like the painful speech he made to a group of wounded soldiers: "You see an envious man. I no longer desire anything on earth except one of your wounds. I salute you, children of France, favorite sons of the Republic, elect who suffer for the fatherland."[5]

As a political figure of considerable importance (even if not such as to be offered dictatorial powers), Hugo was constantly consulted by various civilian and military dignitaries from France and abroad, a role which did not exempt him from his share in the privations of the siege. He too ate rats, dogs, and zoo animals, often composing impromptu poems to ease his and his companions' ingestion of the unknown. The "lover of genius" sought to make up for lost time away from Paris and filled his notebooks with coded references to sexual encounters with a staggering number of women who, sometimes at the rate of several a day, sold or donated their charms to the sixty-eight-year-old poet. The brilliant practitioner of the art of being a grandfather was no less in evidence, recording his grandchildren's development in his journals as assiduously as the details of his liaisons.

This Olympian combination of private and public drama continued when Hugo left Paris after being elected to the new Assembly by the second largest number of votes of all candidates. The Assembly met in Bordeaux, where Hugo went in February 1871, to participate in the painful task of concluding an imposed peace. That task was made even worse by the fact that the Bordeaux Assembly was a new *chambre introuvable* in which Hugo and his fellow republicans were brutally outnumbered by provincial conservatives. The left was not only a minority in the Assembly but was itself hopelessly divided, a situation that led Hugo quickly to resign his position as president of the left caucus.

Within the Assembly, the dominant reactionary delegates consistently attacked Hugo's most cherished beliefs. He responded with his usual eloquence and vigor, and the conflict came to a head on March 8, 1871, when, speaking in defense of Garibaldi's election, Hugo referred to the Italian revolutionary as "the only one of the generals that fought for France who was not defeated."[6] The character of the outburst that statement aroused in the chauvinsitic and conservative body it was addressed to can be readily imagined, but one insult is so memorably stupid that it demands quotation. A vicomte de Lorgeril reacted by insisting that the Assembly "refuse the floor to M. Victor Hugo because he does not speak French."[7] Hooted and scorned, certain that his ideas would always be greeted with insults, Hugo resigned from the Assembly and attempted to return to private family life.

His family was immediately struck by tragedy. On March 13, Charles Hugo, the poet's son and the father of his beloved grandchildren Georges and Jeanne, died of a heart attack. Charles's body, transported to Paris for interment in the family plot at Père Lachaise, arrived on March 18, 1871, the very day the Commune began when the Parisian people defended their cannon against the national army, set up barricades throughout the capital, and forced the regular government to withdraw to Versailles. "L'Enterrement," a poem from *L'Année terrible*, superbly records Hugo's emotions as he accompanied his son's casket through the city of revolutions, his grief shared and respected by a great people in armed insurrection.

After the burial occurred one of the most debated events in a much debated life: Victor Hugo left Paris for Brussels. The ostensible reason, a need to be in Belgium to settle Charles's estate, was probably the actual motive. Charles's affairs were hopelessly entangled, and Hugo's devotion to the welfare of his grandchildren is incontestable. Problems arise because, despite his published intention of returning to Paris as soon as the estate was settled, Hugo made no effort to leave Brussels during the two months of the Commune's existence. The insurrectionary regime was committed to many general principles for which Hugo had long labored, such as social justice or the communal idea itself, and to many specific positions for which he had recently fought, such as rejection of the peace treaty and transformation of the new Assembly. Hugo's works were accordingly an inspiration to many of the Commune's leaders, and a host of reasons could be adduced as to why his presence in Paris was desirable. That it was not accorded has provoked much unfavorable speculation on the poet's political and physical courage, which has in turn elicited many equally speculative defenses of his motivations. Although the reasons for it will undoubtedly never be known with certainty, the absence remains significant. During a civil war in France to which he had deep personal and political connections, Victor Hugo was in Belgium.

While there, he consistently condemned both the Versailles and the Commune governments in the name of the eternally luminous principles which the two sides were equally guilty of violating. "This Commune is as idiotic as the Assembly is ferocious. Insanity on both sides." "It is necessary to hold yourself as on a knife blade between the insanity of the Hôtel de Ville and the insanity of Versailles."[8]

The brutality of those private remarks is missing from the public statements, but the three poems Hugo sent from Brussels for publication during the Commune also invoke a plague on both houses. "Un Cri" and "Pas de représailles" plead for humanly merciful policies, and "Les Deux Monuments" argues against the Commune's planned destruction of the Vendôme column while excoriating the Assembly for bombarding the Arc de Triomphe. Three poems in response to civil war recall the three prose pieces in response to international war, and like the prose, the poetry was nugatory. Not only was the Vendôme column destroyed and the bombardment of Paris intensified, but, during the Bloody Week from May 21 to May 28, 1871, the Commune executed some sixty hostages and the Versailles forces exterminated tens of thousands of rebels in one of the most savage repressions in French history.

Merciless in their slaughter of the men, women, and children who had dared threaten property, the defenders of bourgeois order seemed especially determined to refuse Hugo's pleas for "no reprisals." Belgium's conservatives rushed to support their French brethren by declaring that the Communards

were not political rebels but common criminals; as such, they would be returned
to French justice if they sought refuge in Belgium. Appalled at this inter-
nationalization of the butchery in his homeland, Hugo sent a letter to the
editor of *L'Indépendance Belge* which not only attacked Belgium's position
but set about rectifying it single-handedly: "I am offering this asylum, which
the Belgian government is refusing the vanquished. Where? In Belgium. I am
doing Belgium this honor. I am offering asylum in Brussels."[9] The letter went
on to give Hugo's address and state that anyone presenting himself there, "even
my personal enemy," would be admitted and hence become "inviolable."

The reaction was swift and violent. The night after the letter appeared—
May 27, 1871—a mob which probably included the son of Belgium's minister
of the interior stoned Hugo's house for two hours without police interference.
Jeanne, Hugo's eighteen-month-old granddaughter, was almost struck by a
rock; Georges, his four-year-old grandson, thought the Prussians had come.
After futilely seeking help from their neighbors, the family and servants waited
in terror for an invasion and massacre which seemed imminent. Dawn fortunately dispersed the attackers, however, and an official inquiry began. Its
results were predictable. Hugo, a patent threat to public order, was expelled
from Belgium for life.

Hugo's reproval of the Commune's policies had perplexed the left; his
defense of the Communards' right to mercy nauseated the right. As he departed
from Belgium on June 1, 1871, there was beginning a series of vitriolic attacks
on the poet which would continue for months. One journalist suggested
sending Hugo to P. T. Barnum as a notable freak, another saw him drowning
in "avenging excrement. . . . He is among those who tomorrow will wake up
dead."[10] In a very real sense a man without a country or a party, his beloved
France shamefully defeated from abroad and torn asunder from within, Hugo
left Belgium for Luxembourg. There his horror at the Versailles repression
increased as he heard the stories of fleeing rebels who visited him, particularly
those of Marie Mercier, with whom the sixty-nine-year-old began his passionate
affair during his stay in Luxembourg. Those stories inspired both a deeply felt
series of pleas for amnesty and several of the extraordinary poems dated
"June" in *L'Année terrible*.

After leaving Luxembourg in September 1871 to return to Paris and pursue
the battle for mercy, Hugo saw his efforts come to nothing. The summary
slaughter had stopped, but the legal executions and transportations continued
to decimate the defeated Communards. Except for the at best mediocre
success of briefly delaying Henri Rochefort's removal to the prison colony in
New Caledonia, the poet's labors for the Communards were futile. Moreover,
in an unsuccessful campaign for the Assembly in January 1872, Hugo received
only 96,000 votes, a pitifully small figure compared to the 214,000 he had
received less than a year earlier. The time was out of joint, and virtue and
eloquence could do nothing to put it right. In August 1872, therefore, Hugo

returned to his exile's home in Guernsey, possibly with the idea of a total withdrawal from political life. It was in Guernsey, after two years of political disasters for himself and his country, that Hugo composed *Quatrevingt-Treize*.

As *Quatrevingt-Treize* is an obsessively ambivalent exercise in historical and ahistorical signification, so it stands in a dual relationship to the experiences that preceded its composition. On the one hand, the novel is an escape from the cataclysm of 1870-71, a withdrawal from the Prussian debacle to the days when French armies staggered the world, a refusal of the ambiguities of a revolution in process in the name of a comfortably distant revolution asking awed contemplation instead of direct action. On the other hand, the novel stunningly captures the feel of historical situation, the exhilaration and imperfection of a mass refusing all that had existed before to make and name a previously unimaginable world. The pastoral component of *Quatrevingt-Treize* manifests the repugnant complacency with which *ego Hugo* often viewed, judged, and pronounced on the acts of ordinary mortals. Its historical component demonstrates on the contrary an admirable ability to throw off complacency, look directly at events, and move towards acceptance of a human world not subject to the same processes which bring the dawn every day and the spring every year. The work of a man who knows right from wrong and brooks no dispute on the subject, *Quatrevingt-Treize* simultaneously chronicles the revolutionary overthrow of all such certainty. The novel's contradictions derive from its author's contradictory positions during and after the Commune. Hugo's supercilious aloofness from the muddle of practical politics under-lies the pastoral retreats in *Quatrevingt-Treize*; his unique sensitivity to what the Commune was attempting leads directly to the novel's vindication of the revolutionary need to create new codes for understanding the world. The following discussion will address the affinities between the pastoral component of *Quatrevingt-Treize* and Hugo's experiences in 1870-71 before turning to the historical sensitivity that emerged from the same experiences.

Hugo the novelist used *Quatrevingt-Treize* to rectify history's deafness to Hugo the prophet. If the poet's three calls to the Prussians, French, and Parisians were useless in the real world of 1870, in the fictional world of 1793 the principles those calls voiced are the foundation for the character of Gauvain, whose superhuman military successes belie the defeats regularly following Hugo's oratory. The Bordeaux Assembly may have laughed at stirring appeals for continued resistance to an overpoweringly successful enemy, but Gauvain's ability to win the battle of Dol through a ruse permitting twenty men to overcome and rout an army numbering in the thousands amply demonstrates that no situation is so desperate as to make struggle hopeless. As Hugo wanted his virtue to shine between the insane ferocity of the Commune and Versailles, so Gauvain's purity does shine between the shadowy fanaticism of Lantenac and Cimourdain. "On both sides the same execrable fanfare" is a line from "Un Cri," one of the poems sent from Brussels for publication during the

Commune; it perfectly describes the cacophony to which Republican and Royalist speech sometimes degenerate in *Quatrevingt-Treize*. Cimourdain's dream of Gauvain as the Revolution's undisputed leader suggests Hugo's fantasies of personal dictatorship after the collapse of the Second Empire. Correspondingly, Gauvain's response to the call for deeds higher than political office is reminiscent of the thought with which Hugo consoled himself after the failure of his political dreams: "I do not need to be the civil servant of men. I am the civil servant of God."[11]

The motivation for Hugo's moral stance beyond the exigencies of civil war conforms perfectly to the pastoral vision of *Quatrevingt-Treize*. The novel depicts a conflict between historical and familial duties and makes the eternal light of the sun shine on those characters who affirm the family, as did Hugo when he absented himself from the Paris of the Commune to provide for his daughter-in-law and grandchildren after the death of his son. The Red Cap battalion, Lantenac, and Gauvain do exactly what Hugo did during his stay in Brussels with a newly widowed woman and newly fatherless children: respond to the claims of widow and orphans against the demands of political conflict. The parallels between the Fléchard family, for which the characters of *Quatre-vingt-Treize* remove themselves from history, and the family for which Hugo removed himself from Paris are remarkable. Like Michelle Fléchard in 1793, Alice Hugo in 1871 had just lost her husband and was consequently helpless; two of Michelle Fléchard's three children are named Georgette and René-Jean, a gender reversal of the names of Hugo's grandchildren, Georges and Jeanne. Georgette Fléchard is eighteen months old and about to be weaned when the Red Cap battalion becomes her father, exactly the age and situation of Jeanne Hugo when her grandfather became her father through a comparable transcendence of politics. The extent to which *Quatrevingt-Treize* draws on Hugo's observations of his grandchildren for its depiction of the Fléchard children has often been noted, but the critical connection is less the parallelism in portraiture than the fact that both sets of children motivate a withdrawal from history by men whose duty appears to lie within it.

Many of Hugo's writings during the terrible year are structured around the same foci as pastoral discourse in *Quatrevingt-Treize*: the certainty of basic principles and the granite semantics of their names, the analogy between human and natural activities, the concept of time as cyclical not linear. Like the continual shifts between the languages of flowers and of armies in *Quatre-vingt-Treize*, a profusion of images in the poems of *L'Année terrible* guarantees the concealed sense of history by appeals to the obvious sense of nature.

"Pas de représailles," one of the three poems with a political purpose published under the Commune before appearing in *L'Année terrible*,[12] is also rich in assertions that human meaning is as immutable as nature's. The poem begins by stating that "Je ne fais point fléchir les mots auxquels je crois" and continues by arguing that two kinds of justice are no more conceivable than two suns. If reprisals are ever wrong, then they are always wrong, a truth whose recognition permits the poem to conclude like this: "j'entends rester pur, sans tache et sans puissance. / Je n'abdiquerai pas mon droit à l'innocence." That intriguing identification of the spotless and powerless states, hardly calculated to achieve the poem's ostensible purpose of convincing the leaders of Versailles and Paris to change their policies, defines the right to innocence as a right which must be defended *against* history. The anti-historical orientation of *Quatrevingt-Treize* is an extended elaboration of the same point.

Immediately after Paris began its social revolution in March of 1871, Hugo wrote a poem in praise of the kind of sense making that Gauvain learns, that which is invulnerable to social praxis because it can be accomplished only by the individual conscience.

> Sa conscience est fixe et rien n'y bougera.
> Car, quel que soit le vent qui souffle sur leur flamme,
> Les principes profonds ne tremblent pas dans l'âme;
> Car c'est dans l'infini que leur feu calme luit;
> Car l'ouragan sinistre acharné sur la nuit
> Peut secouer là-haut l'ombre et ses sombres toiles,
> Sans faire dans leurs plis remuer les étoiles.
>
> (*Année terrible*, mars, v)

This stars/principles against storms/events imagery, as common in the writings of 1870-71 as in *Quatrevingt-Treize*, is further evidence of how closely Hugo's concept of immutable truth depends on nature language for its articulation. One of the many poems on children in springtime in *L'Art d'être grand-père*[13] (X, iii) displays the same dependency while explicitly challenging the threat to unvarying truth posed by historical signs.

> Appelez ce doux mois du nom qu'il vous plaira,
> C'est mai, c'est floréal; c'est l'hyménée auguste
> De la chose tremblante et de la chose juste,
> Du nid et de l'azur, du brin d'herbe et du ciel;
> C'est l'heure où tout se sent vaguement éternel;

Regardless of whether we name them by the inherited signs of the *Shepheardes Calander* or the created signs of the Revolutionary calendar, the units of cyclical time are one with the units of morality. Spring is the wedding "de la chose tremblante et de la chose juste," of natural creatures to human categories, and there is nothing that can transform the timeless sense of that blessed union. When nature makes us feel vaguely eternal, it is pointless to represent ourselves as historical.

Gauvain's repudiation of revolutionary imperatives prepared his merger with the dawn by demonstrating that his conscience allowed him to weather

events as a compass steers a ship through the storm. Just after the bloody
repression of the Commune, Hugo used the same image to describe his own
position outside history.

> O beauté de l'aurore! ô majesté de l'astre!
> Gibelin contre Guelfe, Yorck contre Lancastre,
> Capulet, Montaigu, qu'importe! que me font
> Leurs cris, puisque voilà le firmament profond!
> Ame, on a de la place aux voûtes éternelles.
> Le sol manque à nos pieds, non l'azur à nos ailes.
> ....
> Le penseur....
> Il va. Sa conscience est là, rien ne dément
> Cette boussole ayant l'ideal pour aimant.
>
> (*Année terrible*, mai, vi)

Both Hugo and Gauvain believed that "il faut bien quelqu'un qui soit pour
les étoiles" (*Année terrible*, juillet, i) when everyone else is for a party, and
both scorned efforts to devise historical rather than starry ways for doing good.
Pastoral respresentation in *Quatrevingt-Treize* is identical to the vision of the
world which sustained Hugo's battles and motivated his retreats throughout
the years surrounding the novel's composition.

There are of course different ways to evaluate Hugo's moral behavior during
the Commune. Either we can see the noble conviction of a prophet in his
determination to stand "not with a party but with a principle"[14] and in the
vociferous blasts he directed at all parties that violated principles. Or we can
see the stubborn rigidity of an egomaniac destroying Hugo's ability to work
effectively for principles by portraying himself as the world's only pure man
so constantly as to destroy in less than a year a popularity and respect second
to none in Europe. The lengthy list of works assessing Hugo's activities during
the terrible year contains examples of both extremes and most positions in
between. The passions of 1871 were extremely durable in France, and the
books on Hugo's positions which began to appear in that year set a rapid pace
and a belligerent tone that would continue for decades. Without attempting
to choose among the different interpretations of Hugo's remaining above the
fray, let me simply state here that, however we interpret them, the poet's
political statements in 1870 and 1871 are substantive and formal precursors of
the pastoral components of *Quatrevingt-Treize*. In the novel as in the world,
the stars draw humanity away from its history.

The biographical origin of historical representation in *Quatrevingt-Treize*,
of those passages which express human not astral commitment, is equally
significant but more difficult to document. An undercurrent in Hugo's public
and private writings suggests a certain discomfort with his solitary devotion to
divine justice at a time when the people of Paris were collectively struggling
and dying to institute social justice. It is consistent with *ego Hugo*'s antipathy

for self-recrimination that doubts concerning his first assessment of the Commune never take the form of developed admissions of error. His most coherent and extensive statement that history may be something other than progress toward transhistorical goals is in fact the vision of the French Revolution in *Quatrevingt-Treize*. Nevertheless, the events of 1871 are the conditions of possibility for that vision, and Hugo's conscious assessments of the Commune and its defenders suggest an unconsciously increasing feeling for what revolution means. The Commune was a social laboratory in which something wholly new, something previously unrepresentable because previously unimaginable, was being created. Hugo's blindness to this newness became with time a remarkable openness to acts which radically and rudely called into question his concept of univocal human purpose.

The presumption that Hugo began to doubt the absolute truth of his political principles is in part authorized by the cold fact that they were bathetically inefficacious during the terrible year. The poet-philosopher was always subject to confusing the particular effects of his situation in time and space with the human race's eternal condition, a flight from the individual to the universal particularly apparent in his unheeded paeans to Paris and France during and after the Prussian invasion. The myth of Paris as the capital of mankind, a dominant theme in the writings of 1870-71, was a lived belief as well as a rhetorical device. On September 1, 1870, for example, immediately before departing for Paris after twenty years of exile, Hugo wrote Paul Meurice that he was returning because "to defend Paris is to defend the world. *Homo sum*, therefore I defend Paris."[15] Explicit identification of Paris with the world leads to the adoption of Latin, the transnational and transhistorical language, in allusion to Terence's celebrated *Homo sum, humani nil a me alienum puto*. Hugo's substitution of "I defend Paris" for "I consider nothing human alien to me" affirms an equivalency between one city and Western humanism which was for him as incontestable as the eternity of moral principles.

Like Hugo's call to the Germans, several poems in *L'Année terrible* are based on France's identity with the universe. To take only one example, "A qui la victoire définitive?" (décembre, ix) equates the "French goal" with the "human goal" and contains a variant demonstrating with particular force Hugo's confusion of patriotism with universality. The final text calls on the Germans to respect "la vérité, vraie à toute heure, en tout lieu." The original version of that line summoned respect for "l'avenir qu'emplit la *Marseillaise* en feu."

The difficulty with the representational system in which eternal truth substitutes for a national anthem and patriotic devotion to a city is synonymous with humanistic universality was the brutal regularity with which events demonstrated its inadequacy to the world. The French in 1871 respected Hugo's vision of an inviolable capital of the universe no more than did the Prussians in 1870. Even for solitary visionaries who listen to God, that kind of contradiction between reality and its encoding can instill the suspicion that codes are arbitrary.

The same contradiction undermined Hugo's idealistic concept of revolution, whose close connection to his vision of Paris is apparent in his speech to the colossal crowd greeting the exile's return.

> To save Paris is more than to save France, it is to save the world. Paris is the very center of humanity. Paris is the sacred city. Who attacks Paris attacks in mass the entire human race. Paris is the capital of civilization. And do you know why Paris is the city of civilization? It is because Paris is the city of revolution.[16]

This use of "revolution" in September of 1870 is identical to that made during the Commune in one of Hugo's most quoted pronouncements. "All my thought oscilates between two poles: Civilization, Revolution. When freedom is in peril, I say: Civilization, but Revolution; when it is order that is in danger, I say: Revolution, but Civilization."[17] These couplings of "civilization" and "revolution" are also found in the Olympian judgements of *Quatrevingt-Treize* (e.g., p. 202). In both contexts, they betray a pre-1792 understanding of revolution. The Paris of the sections demonstrated that "civilization" is another word for the old order and that the effect of revolution is to explode order and thus make possible new thoughts of what is civilized. If the Paris Commune was in some ways a prisoner of the Great Revolution's goals and institutions, one of the ways it was an active successor instead of a passive emulator was in its constantly increasing capacity to reject a social system formally equated with civilization itself. For Marx, the Commune was a "completely new historical creation"[18] which, against all concepts of what was feasible or even thinkable, established a system in which "plain working men for the first time dared to infringe upon the governmental privilege of their 'natural superiors.' "[19] That Hugo was for a time insensitive to the fact that the Commune's progress toward authentic revolution necessarily involved violation of what was "natural" and "civilized" is far less startling than his eventual ability to correct his error. The man who in *Quatrevingt-Treize* presented revolution as the necessarily bloody destruction of the old world and the necessarily unimaginable overthrow of old representations of it had developed far beyond the man who in 1871 argued that "la révolution n'est autre chose que la révolution faite à l'amiable."[20]

Like the ideas of amicable revolutions and static civilizations, Hugo's concept that all principles are immutable had to be challenged before *Quatrevingt-Treize* could become the text it is. The poet's originally negative assessment of the Commune was part and parcel of his essentialist vision of human activity, which made it possible for him to reject and ignore historical facts that did not live up to his view of what history should be. The same letter that describes a thought oscillating between civilization and revolution, for example, asserts that politics is progress toward a great goal given in advance.

Because the Commune is moving toward different goals, its acts are the "nega-tion of principles" and it itself is separate from the Paris that made it.[21] Such statements are consistent with the thought patterns of Hugo's entire life, and it was consequently necessary for him to wrench himself free of his most deeply rooted categories before he could sense the validity of the Commune's effort to invent principles to replace those it was negating.

Part of the wrenching process was accomplished by the uninterrupted dichotomy between the sterling principle of nonviolence and the reality of the terrible year. The gross incongruousness of Hugo's public appeals for fraternity was matched by the catastrophic effects of his private counsel. After the insurgence of January 22, 1871, for instance, Gustave Flourens came to ask Hugo's advice. The sage's response was "No violent pressure on the situation,"[22] an irreproachable sentiment in the abstract but one whose inapplicability to a city preparing for social war was brought home by the fact that Flourens was arrested while leaving Hugo's house. Condemned to death for his part in the October 31 rebellion and summarily executed by a Versailles officer during the Commune, Flourens had little reason to admire Hugo's wisdom during the two months of life that remained to him after his quest for advice.

Flourens' murder was the first of many deaths of people who in one way or another had listened to Hugo's dreams. The extraordinary journal entry of June 3, 1871, suggests the extent of the shock such deaths administered: "Cournet shot, Razoua shot, Delescluze killed, Millière shot, Ranc imprisoned, Ed. Lockroy imprisoned, were part of the left caucus which I presided over in the Sieuzac house in Bordeaux. That was three months ago."[23] Hugo's constant policy in discussing politics was to "invite everyone to calm and union."[24] Since so many of the delegates who chose him as their president in February had by June been taught most forcefully that calm and union were goals shared rather less than universally, it seems legitimate to assume that Hugo was beginning to learn the same lesson. The list of jailed and executed comrades eloquently poses a question that is not made overt; both its eloquence and its reticence are typical of the journal entries following France's bloody repression of Paris.

Hugo's own protest against that repression, his personal offer of asylum to fleeing Communards, was made *"pro jure contra legem."*[25] It provoked a violent assault on his home and his family by men equally indifferent to law but with a wildly different understanding of right. The effect of that challenge to Hugo's universalist morality is directly related to the vacillating significance which *Quatrevingt-Treize* attaches to the [+human] semantic feature. Hugo made his offer of asylum in opposition to a decree by a minister who declared that Belgian soil must be preserved from "people who barely deserve the name of men."[26] The effect of such a statement on Hugo, for whom man was always and everywhere himself as surely as Paris was his capital, was immediate and immense. Like Tellmarch, he saw men as men and believed that they invariably

deserved respect: "Résistez, quel que soit le nom dont il se nomme, / A qui-
conque vous donne un conseil contre l'homme" (Année terrible, mai, iii). Yet,
again like Tellmarch, Hugo saw his principles come into sudden conflict with
activity which refuted the truism of man's identity with himself. Like Tellmarch's
doubts about whether Lantenac is part of the human race, Hugo's poem on the
attack against his house, "Une Nuit à Bruxelles" (Année terrible, mai, v),
dehumanizes humans when it describes the attackers as creatures whose voices
"n'avaient plus rien d'humain." The real stones thrown at a sick baby had the
same effect as the imagined massacre of Herbe-en-Pail, violent contradiction
of a world view in which humanity is humane.

And in "Une Nuit à Bruxelles" as in Quatrevingt-Treize, the refuge from
history's turbulence is pastoral certitude. If no human beings respond to calls
for help, the trees on the square tremble with indignation; if adults are beasts,
children are angels who comfort one another. "Une Nuit à Bruxelles" concludes
with a line that abruptly abandons the chronicle of human perfidy and sets the
reader in the superior world of natural beauty: "Et j'entendais au loin chanter
un rossignol."

After the nocturnal attack, Hugo continued to prefer birds' songs to men's
meanings. Expelled from Brussels by Leopold III, Hugo magisterially scorned
his persecutor as a "third-order king" and, in the poem with that title (La Corde
d'airain, ix), described the contempt for political activity imparted to him by
God's gloriously unsullied world.

> Les injures qu'on peut me faire sont couvertes
> Par l'azur, par le doux frisson des branches vertes,
> Par le divin babil des nids mélodieux.[27]

Nature's availability makes history immaterial, so, after their forced departure
from Belgium, Hugo and his family abandoned the stage of the great powers
for tiny Luxembourg. They arrived in the rural tranquility of Vianden on
June 8, 1871, hoping to find in God's world a niche which seemed to have
been denied them in man's.

But history followed in the form of continuous new information on what
the Commune had tried to do and how it had been obliterated, an invasion
of Arcadia which may be the most crucial event of the entire terrible year.
If the source of the authentically revolutionary vision in Quatrevingt-Treize
can be biographically localized, it must be set in the few weeks at Vianden
when nature failed and history so insistently drew attention to itself that
Hugo's eyes were opened to something they had never seen before, the relativity
of what an age calls civilization and the viability of a revolution against it.

The transformation began with the sensations described in "A Vianden"
(Année terrible, juin, xiv), written the day of Hugo's arrival. Nature's beauteous magnificence has become powerless to divert thoughts from society.

Il songe. Il s'est assis rêveur sous un érable.
Entend-il murmurer la forêt vénérable?
Regarde-t-il les fleurs? Regarde-t-il les cieux?
Il songe. La nature au front mystérieux
Fait tout ce qu'elle peut pour apaiser les hommes;
Du coteau plein de vigne au verger plein de pommes
Les mouches viennent, vont, reviennent; les oiseaux
Jettent leur petite ombre errante sur les eaux. . . .

Twenty-five more lines memorably depict the glory of a rural scene before the concluding revelation that none of this splendor matters. The dreamer cannot become one with nature while "on fait consumer en hâte par la chaux / Des corps d'hommes sanglants et d'enfants encor chauds."

Although the ahistorical sensation of pity causes the impotence of the pastoral vision in "A Vianden," the poem points toward legitimately historical understanding. Because it insulates both nature's grandeur and morality's certainty from human action, pastoral representation permits indifference to the world in the name of something higher. No matter how stormy mankind's deeds may become, meanwhile and nevertheless the sun rises in glorious confirmation of the principles which set right-thinking people above the turbulence. To close off the escape offered by the sun for whatever reason is to open the possibility of a unilaterally historical existence in which human events are experienced from on earth rather than judged from on high. The skies formerly called the poet away from the turpitude of inferior beings; the agony of the Commune reverses that process by calling him down from the skies.

In Vianden, the compassion Hugo always felt for the defeated developed into awareness that the Communards' *historical* situation had shut them off from humanity's *eternal* condition. "A qui la faute?" (*Année terrible*, juin, viii) at length attacks a rebel for the infamous and impious crime of burning a library before concluding with the arsonist's eloquently brief rebuttal, "I don't know how to read," a conclusion that effectively destroys Hugo's cherished idea of a continuum between what passed for civilization and what revolution had to be. The superb "Les Fusillés" (*Année terrible*, juin, xii) goes even further by suggesting that enjoyment of springtime is as socially restricted an activity as perusal of the classics. The poem considers the sinister ease in dying—"cette facilité sinistre de mourir"—displayed by rebels captured while defending their right to a different world and broaches the possibility that socioeconomic oppression invalidates the most beneficent of nature's gifts.

Donc ils ne tiennent pas à la vie; elle est faite
De façon qu'il leur est égal de s'en aller.
C'est en plein mois de mai; tout veut vivre et mêler
Son instinct ou son âme à la douceur des choses;
Ces filles-là devraient aller cueillir des roses;

> L'enfant devrait jouer dans un rayon vermeil;
> L'hiver de ce vieillard devrait fondre au soleil;
> Ces âmes devraient être ainsi que des corbeilles
> S'emplissant de parfums, de murmures d'abeilles,
> De chants d'oiseaux, de fleurs, d'extase, de printemps!
> Tous devraient être d'aube et d'amour palpitants.
> Eh bien, dans ce beau mois de lumière et d'ivresse,
> O terreur! c'est la mort qui brusquement se dresse. . . .

Style and imagery are here very close to the pastoral sections of *Quatrevingt-Treize*, which evoke the "douceur colossale des choses" (p. 346) as lyrically as this poem describes the "douceur des choses." But in "Les Fusillés" historical fact directly invalidates the vision only threatened by the Revolution in *Quatrevingt-Treize*. Pastoral's universalist perspective generates the unequivocal statement that "everything wants to live" in things' sweetness. History immediately contradicts that belief and converts the poem's verb tenses from the eternal present to a wistful conditional, repeated five times in a melancholy recital of what "ought to be" but is not. The stock language of bucolic bliss, filled "de chants d'oiseaux, de fleurs, d'extase, de printemps!" is empty verbiage as alien to the narrative of death for social liberation as was the birds' small wandering shadow to the meditations of a man unable to forget that those deaths were occurring. The June poems of *L'Année terrible* make poignantly clear that the sun is rising meanwhile and nevertheless; they are equally eloquent in asking how anybody could care.

Refusal of pastoral time complements rejection of pastoral values. The global structure of *L'Année terrible* excludes the sensation of cyclical events by sweeping the reader from month to month in an irreversible progress perfectly suited to emphasizing the nonpertinence of God's seasons to man's world.

> J'écris ce livre, jour par jour, sous la dictée
> De l'heure qui se dresse et fuit épouvantée;
> Les semaines de l'An Terrible sont autant
> D'hydres que l'enfer crée et que le gouffre attend;
> L'événement s'en va, roulant des yeux de flamme,
> Après avoir posé sa griffe sur mon âme.
>
> *(Année terrible*, avril, iii)

It was at Vianden that the collection of poems on the history of a year first received the name that proclaimed its historical nature, *L'Année terrible*. The many earlier titles—*Paris héroïque, Paris combattant, Paris martyr, Le Drame de Paris, L'Epopée de Paris*—had all designated the myth of Paris instead of the reality of events, and that myth too melted in the heat of the stories heard at Vianden.

A more significant myth which tumbled in June of 1871 was that which conflates a peculiar social organization with a timeless "right to property." The condemnation of the Commune as the insane aberration of uncivilized savages by a continent relatively unconcerned with Versailles's barbaric executions is revealing evidence that violence to things terrified the nineteenth-century bourgeoisie incomparably more than violence to persons. While Hugo was in Brussels, he seemed to share this general perversion of his age and class. His notebooks contain very few condemnations of the dispatch with which M. Thiers's forces butchered their prisoners, but the Communards' actions against property elicited entries like this: "The Commune is having Thiers's house demolished. Odious and stupid."[28] When the rebels in defeat set fire to the monuments of the capital of the universe, Hugo's stupefaction was as great as that of his contemporaries. Several poems assault the inconceivable monstrosity of such a deed, so heinous that Hugo's first reaction on hearing of it was to reject it as incompatible with the ways of the world.[29] In brief, Hugo was at first a full-fledged member of the bourgeoisie which Marx scorned for being "convulsed by horror at the desecration of brick and mortar"[30] effected by the Commune.

At Vianden, Hugo rose above the perspective of his class to recognize the historical cause of material destruction. "Les Fusillés" contains this remarkable section.

> Et n'ont-ils pas eu froid? et n'ont-ils pas eu faim?
> C'est pour cela qu'ils ont brûlé vos Tuileries.
> Je le déclare au nom de ces âmes meurtries,
> Moi, l'homme exempt des deuils de parade et d'emprunt,
> Qu'un enfant mort émeut plus qu'un palais défunt.

"Defunct palace" is surprising, "*your* Tuileries" astounding. One month after being wholly unable to believe that Paris was burning, Hugo repudiated one of the glories of the sacred city in the name of a dead child and an oppressed class.

Hugo's evolving perspectives on the Commune provoked an even more agonizing reassessment of its leaders, who had regularly pricked the poet's vanity by ignoring his morally and rhetorically impeccable advice. The most fascinating illustration is the development of journal references to Charles Delescluze, the most important spokesman for neo-Jacobins haunted by the legend of 1793, when gods and kings were swept away by an irresistible surge of the popular will. The neo-Jacobins were one among many factions in the disparate conglomeration of ideologies brought together under the Commune, and Delescluze was in large measure out of touch with what was in fact radically new in 1871, Paris's creation of a working-class government and tentative steps toward a working-class society. On the other hand, as an anti-Girondin

admirer of the Committee of Public Safety, Delescluze was equally distant
from the proto-*gauchiste* elements in the Commune, those who resisted revolutionary discipline and organization in the name of individual and communal
autonomy. One of the spokesmen for the latter faction, Jules Vallès, perceived
Delescluze as lost and alone at the first session of the newly elected Commune.

> He was out of his element among all these workclothes and all this insubordina-
> tion. . . . And this veteran of classical revolution, the legendary prison hero who,
> having been in on the suffering, wanted to be in on the honor as well, thought
> himself entitled to two inches of dais and found himself at ground level with no
> one looking at him with particular interest, with everyone listening to him perhaps
> less than to Clément, the dyer, who had come from Vaugirard in clogs.
>
> I felt pity and respect before the sadness he could not hide. It made me suffer
> to see him trying to double his stride to keep up with the federals' accelerated
> pace; his will was running out of breath and bleeding in its attempt to join the
> marching Commune.
>
> His effort was a complete confession, an act of penance, a silent and heroic
> admission of thirty years of injustice to those he had treated as troublemakers, even
> as traitors, because they were moving faster than his Old Man of the Mountain
> committee.[31]

I have quoted that long passage to display an identity and a distinction
between Delescluze and Hugo. The identity is that both men saw the Commune
as opposed to principles for which they had argued and fought for decades and
that both experienced this opposition as a personal affront. The distinction is
that Delescluze, "silent and heroic," devoted himself to a revolution which in
large part he did not understand; Hugo, loquacious and secure, went to
Belgium.

The relationship between the poet and the revolutionary was similarly
complex long before the Commune. Both were violently opposed to the
Second Empire and both suffered for their resistance, Hugo by exile, Delescluze
by prison and transportation. (His experiences during the latter were the ghastly
horrors which Zola makes part of Florent's story in *Le Ventre de Paris*.) Their
alliance against the common enemy, Napoleon III, was strained when Hugo,
thundering his famous "If only one remains, I will be that one," refused to
return from exile in order to do what Delescluze saw as the republican duty
of practical activity against the regime from within the country. Delescluze
criticized Hugo's aloofness with amusing and accurate irony, advising the
sage to continue "directing, from the peak of his rock, the course of worlds
and the sun."[32] Delescluze himself preferred to abandon purity for rebellion.

Hugo and Delescluze did not actually meet until 1871 when, after both
were elected to the Bordeaux Assembly, Delescluze was a member of the left
caucus under Hugo's presidency. They seem to have had no major differences
on policy, but something about Delescluze's person irritated Hugo beyond
measure and stimulated private swipes in his journals like this: "As for

M. Delescluze, we have only one word to say to him: We scorn him. It would not displease me if that displeased him."[33] After Hugo's resignation as a delegate, he and Delescluze separated again; the latter, true to his principle of attacking from within, did not resign from the Assembly until after the first session of the Commune.

It was consequently with many personal and political motives for disapproval that Hugo observed Delescluze's activities from Brussels, a disapproval evident throughout the poet's remarks on the Commune. In a highly unusual quotation of someone else's words in his journal, for example, Hugo entered this catty characterization of Delescluze as old and envious: "il est né vieux et envieux."[34] Delescluze's concept of political duty, the direct opposite of Hugo's, insisted on practical activity despite the compromise of principle it might entail. Accordingly, when some members of the Commune resigned because they felt their ideals being violated, Delescluze renounced his own objections to the course the revolution was taking and made the following remarks:

> For personal bitterness or because the ideal pursued is not in accord with the project, we must not withdraw. Do you believe that everyone approves what is done here? Well, there are members who have remained and who will remain until the end despite the insults heaped on us. As for me, I am determined to stay at my post and, if we do not see victory, we will not be the last to be struck.[35]

Hugo's reaction to the statement that people must not withdraw when the "ideal pursued is not in accord with the project" can be readily imagined. Translating his moral objections into personal contempt, he made the following comment on Delescluze's declaration: "Citizen Delescluze declares that he will not abandon the Commune and *that he will let himself be killed*. I doubt it" [Hugo's emphasis].[36]

But Delescluze gave the lie to Hugo's doubt in an extraordinarily heroic manner. At the end of Bloody Week, after it became clear that the Commune was defeated and that he no longer had the duty of organizing the defense, Delescluze walked over a barricade toward the attacking Versailles forces, calmly inviting a death which immediately came. Lissagaray, still the best historian of the Commune, witnessed Delescluze's death and movingly commented on it.

> He had informed no one, not even his most intimate friends. Silent, confiding only in his severe conscience, Delescluze walked to the barricade as the old Montagnards went to the guillotine. The long day of his life had spent his strength. Only a breath remained to him; he gave it. He lived only for justice. . . . A Jacobin, he fell with socialists to defend it. It was his compensation to die for it, his hands free, in the sun, at his time, without being afflicted by the sight of the executioner.[37]

In an alteration of his journal which is in its way as great a tribute as Lissagaray's eulogy, Hugo turned back the pages to cross out the "I doubt it" with which he had glossed Delescluze's vow to die for the Commune.

It is of course impossible to know exactly when that eloquent crossing-out took place. What is certain is that, at least two weeks after learning of Delescluze's death and immediately before making the stunning repudiation of Parisian monuments in "Les Fusillés," Hugo was still pondering the man to whom he had formerly had only one thing to say, that he scorned him. The journal entries for Vianden contain this long résumé of Hugo's contact with Delescluze.

> At Bordeaux, Charles Delescluze was part of the left representatives' caucus in rue Lafaurie-Monbadon where I was president. I had never seen him. One day, at a session unusually held in the daytime, I spotted at the end of the table where we were sitting a livid profile, yellow eyes, bilious lips, white hair formerly blond. Edouard Lockroy was at my right. I said to him, "Which man is that?" He answered me softly, "It's Delescluze." The question was Alsace's representatives. . . . Delescluze spoke for [my proposal] in the same tone he would have used to speak against. He affected not to pronounce my name and designated me thus: *the citizen*. Which did not bother me. He looked at me with inexpressible hatred in his eyes. That evening, there was another meeting on the same subject. . . . Delescluze got up, his face sinister and furious, looked at my proposition on the desk and declared with rage that he approved it. I saw him only those two times.[38]

It is necessary to bear *ego Hugo*'s personality in mind to appreciate the extent to which that string of insults is also a *mea culpa*. The passage has the tone of a most uncomfortable effort to explain away a contempt that events have belied. For example, it is certain that being called the "citizen" in fact deeply wounded Hugo's vanity. Among the aspects of the expulsion from Belgium which most upset the bearer of a world-renowned name was that one of his persecutors persisted in designating him as the "individual," and his journal entries almost always contemptuously refer to his Jacobin enemy as "citizen Delescluze." The announcement that the revolutionary title did not bother him when it bothered him very much points to the same inference as the constant references to Delescluze's antipathy for him when it is his for Delescluze that is certainly at issue. Although the closest he could come to admitting it was to catalogue the reasons for his mistake, while at Vianden Hugo began to suspect that his original assessment of Delescluze and all the Communards who pursued a project instead of an ideal was seriously in error.

Escape from the discomfort that near confession produced came through the reassuring thought that Victor Hugo is the kind of man who does not hurt even big hairy spiders. As in *Quatrevingt-Treize*, mercy is above all political questions. Immediately after almost confronting a thorny reassessment of his political behavior, Hugo retreated to thoughts of an event which proved his transcendent pity. The long meditation on Delescluze leads to the unusual step of promoting a mundane incident of everyday life to the status of a journal entry: "I saw him only those two times. This morning I found a fat spider in my wash basin. It was really scared. I did not hurt it."[39] That passage offers relief from political doubt by supplying evidence of apolitical mercy, a pattern which conforms to the general shifts of Hugo's thought after the Commune's eradication. For the same reasons that *Quatrevingt-Treize* is an antihistorical work, Hugo could never fully admit the Commune's right to destroy the old world in order to create a new society. But for the same reason that *Quatrevingt-Treize* incorporates the open form of revolutionary meaning, Hugo's references to the Commune also display the capacity to emerge from the vision of the world imposed by bourgeois society despite the philosophical and psychological impediments to such a liberation.

In a letter to Kugelman written on April 12, 1871, Marx described the Communards as "those Parisians storming heaven" who had established "a new point of departure of world-historical importance."[40] Hugo was incapable of accepting the negation of principles and of the pastorally static forms which represent them implicit in the idea that heaven is something human beings can storm. Heaven is after all where the eternal stars shine brightly despite the clouds that may hide them from those on earth. Nevertheless, Hugo was alone among respected authors in the extent to which he came to accept the Communards' right to struggle against the clouds enveloping them regardless of their disturbance of heavenly tranquility. In his life as in *Quatrevingt-Treize*, Hugo at least entertained the thought that history can transmute good and evil into their opposites. "A new point of departure of world-historical importance" is beyond the reach of inherited forms of thought; pastoral discourse is unable to express what authentic revolutions attempt to do. The dual, conflicting forms of representation in *Quatrevingt-Treize* emerge from Hugo's obsessively conflicting perceptions of the Commune, simultaneously a storm to be repelled in the name of heaven and a new human possibility to be pondered in the name of history.

Notes

[Whenever material in English is referenced with a French source, the translation is by Sandy Petrey.]

Introduction

[1] Karl Marx, *The Eighteenth Brumaire of Louis Bonaparte* (New York: International Publishers, 1963), p. 15.

[2] Georg Lukács, *Studies in European Realism* (New York: Grosset and Dunlap, 1964), p. 27. All further references to this work appear in the text with the abbreviation *SER*.

[3] Julia Kristeva, *La Révolution du langage poétique* (Paris: Seuil, 1974), p. 61. All further references to this work appear in the text with the abbreviation *RLP*.

[4] Balzac, letter to Eve Hanska, June 26, 1847, quoted in *Les Paysans* (Paris: Garnier, 1964), p. xiii.

[5] Leo Bersani, *A Future for Astyanax* (Boston: Little, Brown, 1976), pp. 60-61.

[6] Emile Benveniste, *Problèmes de linguistique générale*, 2 vols. (Paris: Gallimard, 1966, 1974), II, Ch. 6.

[7] Quoted in Ferdinand Brunot, *Histoire de la langue française des origines à 1900* (Paris: Colin, 1937), IX, 691.

[8] Quoted in Brunot, p. 683.

[9] Quoted in Brunot, p. vii.

[10] Quoted in Brunot, p. v.

[11] Quoted in Brunot, p. 1157.

[12] Quoted in Brunot, p. 907.

[13] Quoted in Alphonse Aulard, *Paris pendant la réaction thermidorienne et sous le Directoire* (Paris: Cerf, 1898), I, 567.

14 Phillipe-Joseph-Benjamin Buchez and Prosper-Charles Roux, *Histoire parlementaire de la révolution française*, 40 vols. (Paris: Paulin, 1834-38), XXIV, 420.

15 Quoted in Brunot, p. 655.

16 Thomas Carlyle, *The French Revolution* (New York: Modern Library, 1934), pp. 634-35.

Chapter 1: Children Belong with Their Mother

1 Erich Auerbach, *Mimesis* (New York: Doubleday, 1953), p. 401.

2 Quoted in Léon Moussinac, *Eisenstein* (New York: Crown, 1970), pp. 84-85.

3 Benveniste, I, Ch. 19.

4 Victor Hugo, *Quatrevingt-Treize* (Paris: Garnier, 1963), p. 255. All further references to this work appear in the text.

5 Albert Camus, *The Myth of Sisyphus* (New York: Vintage, 1960), p. 5.

Chapter 3: Pastoral and Historical Discourse

1 Michael Riffaterre, "Interpretation and Descriptive Poetry: A Reading of Wordsworth's 'Yew-Trees,' " *New Literary History*, 4 (1972-73), 230.

2 Michael Riffaterre, "L'Explication des faits littéraires," in *L'Enseignement de la littérature*, ed. Serge Doubrovsky and Tzvetan Todorov (Paris: Plon, 1971), pp. 354-55.

3 Tzvetan Todorov, *Introduction à la littérature fantastique* (Paris: Seuil, 1970), p. 37.

4 Quoted in Hugo, *Quatrevingt-Treize*, pp. ix, xvii.

5 Ferdinand de Saussure, *Course in General Linguistics* (New York: McGraw-Hill, 1959), p. 117.

6 William Empson, *Some Versions of Pastoral* (New York: New Directions, 1960), p. 254.

7 Peter Marinelli, *Pastoral* (London: Methuen, 1971), p. 11.

8 Adolphe Thiers, *The History of the French Revolution* (London: Bentley, 1881), III, 256.

9 The three quotations are, in order of presentation: Nicolas Boileau, *Œuvres complètes*, ed. Françoise Escal (Paris: Pléiade, 1966), p. 163; Alexander Pope, *Pastoral Poetry and An Essay on Criticism*, ed. E. Audra and A. Williams (New Haven: Yale Press, 1961), pp. 25-27; and Samuel Johnson, *Lives of the Poets: A Selection*, ed. J. P. Hardy (Oxford: Clarendon, 1971), p. 285.

[10] Paul Fussell, *The Great War and Modern Memory* (New York: Oxford, 1975), Ch. 7.

[11] Tadeusz Borowski, *This Way for the Gas, Ladies and Gentlemen* (New York: Penguin, 1976), p. 100.

[12] Borowski, p. 132.

[13] Claude Lévi-Strauss, *The Savage Mind* (Chicago: University of Chicago Press, 1966), pp. 233-35.

[14] Letter to Edgar Quinet, March 2, 1874, quoted in *Quatrevingt-Treize*, p. i.

[15] See Chapter 3, note 4.

Chapter 4: Il y a des mots qui font vivre

[1] Quoted in Pierre Larousse, *Grand Dictionaire universel*, 17 vols. (Paris: Larousse, 1865-90), II, 825.

[2] Brunot, p. 951.

[3] Quoted in Larousse, XII, 406.

[4] Quoted in Gérard Walter, *La Révolution française* (Paris: Charpentier, 1967), p. 118.

[5] Quoted in Buchez and Roux, XX, 423.

[6] Quoted in Buchez and Roux, XV, 42.

[7] Quoted in Brunot, p. 640.

[8] See Albert Soboul, *Les Sans-culottes parisiens de l'An II* (Paris: Clavreuil, 1958), pp. 650-53.

[9] Quoted in Soboul, p. 561.

[10] Quoted in Soboul, p. 1074.

[11] In *The Structuralists from Marx to Lévi-Strauss*, ed. Richard and Fernande DeGeorge (New York: Anchor, 1972), pp. 85-122.

[12] Fussell, p. 231.

[13] Quoted in Brunot, p. 690.

[14] Quoted in Brunot, p. 691.

[15] Quoted in Soboul, p. 655.

Chapter 5: Can a Good Deed Be a Bad Deed?

1 Jules Vallès, *The Insurrectionist* (Englewood Cliffs: Prentice-Hall, 1971), p. 210.

2 Plato, *Selections*, ed. Raphael Demos (New York: Scribners, 1955), p. 267.

Chapter 7: Those Parisians Storming Heaven

1 R. R. Palmer, introd., *The Coming of the French Revolution*, by Georges Lefebvre (New York: Vintage, 1960), p. ix.

2 Victor Hugo, *Carnets intimes, 1870-1871*, ed. Henri Guillemin (Paris: Gallimard, 1953), p. 205.

3 Victor Hugo, *Œuvres complètes*, 18 vols. (Paris: Club français du livre, 1967-71), XV, 1240.

4 Hugo, *Carnets*, p. 41.

5 Hugo, *Carnets*, pp. 65-66.

6 Hugo, *Œuvres complètes*, XV, 1271.

7 Quoted in Hugo, *Œuvres complètes*, XV, 1272.

8 Hugo, *Carnets*, pp. 125, 273.

9 Quoted in Victor Hugo, *Œuvres poétiques*, ed. Pierre Albouy, III (Paris: Pléiade, 1974), 1065.

10 Quoted in Hugo, *Œuvres complètes*, XV, 1215.

11 Hugo, *Carnets*, p. 206.

12 Hugo, *Œuvres complètes*, XV, 17-226.

13 Hugo, *Œuvres complètes*, XV, 857-990.

14 Hugo, *Carnets*, p. 221.

15 Hugo, *Œuvres complètes*, XIV, 1312.

16 Hugo, *Œuvres complètes*, XV, 1239.

17 Hugo, *Œuvres complètes*, XV, 1289.

18 Karl Marx, *The Civil War in France* (Peking: Foreign Languages Press, 1970), p. 70.

19 Marx, *Civil War*, p. 74.

[20] Hugo, *Œuvres complètes*, XVI, 974.

[21] Hugo, *Œuvres complètes* XV, 1289.

[22] Hugo, *Carnets*, p. 96.

[23] Hugo, *Carnets*, p. 143.

[24] Hugo, *Carnets*, p. 96.

[25] Quoted in Hugo, *Œuvres poétiques*, III, 1065.

[26] Quoted in Hugo, *Œuvres poétiques*, III, 1064.

[27] Hugo, *Œuvres poétiques*, III. 528.

[28] Hugo, *Carnets*, p. 135.

[29] Hugo, *Carnets*, p. 137.

[30] Marx, *Civil War*, p. 93.

[31] Vallès, pp. 178-79.

[32] Marcel Dassal, *Un Révolutionnaire jacobin, Charles Delescluze* (Paris: Marcel Rivière, 1952), p. 253.

[33] Hugo, *Carnets*, p. 212.

[34] Hugo, *Carnets*, p. 133.

[35] Quoted in Prosper Lissagaray, *Histoire de la Commune de 1871* (Paris: Librairie du Travail, 1929), p. 207.

[36] Hugo, *Carnets*, p. 129.

[37] Lissagaray, p. 356.

[38] Hugo, *Carnets*, pp. 151-52.

[39] Hugo, *Carnets*, p. 152.

[40] Karl Marx, *The Civil War in France* (New York: International Publishers, 1968). pp. 86-87.

Selected Bibliography

Albouy, Pierre. *Mythographies*. Paris: Corti, 1976.

Auerbach, Erich. *Mimesis*. Trans. Willard Trask. New York: Doubleday, 1953.

Aulard, Alphonse. *Paris pendant la réaction thermidorienne et sous le Directoire*. Paris: Cerf, 1898. Vol I.

de Balzac, Honoré. *Les Paysans*. Ed. Jean Hervé Donnard. Paris: Garnier, 1964.

Benveniste, Emile. *Problèmes de linguistique générale*. 2 vols. Paris: Gallimard, 1966, 1974.

Bersani, Leo. *A Future for Astyanax*. Boston: Little, Brown, 1976.

Boileau, Nicolas. *Œuvres complètes*. Ed. Françoise Escal. Paris: Pléiade, 1966.

Borowski, Tadeusz. *This Way for the Gas, Ladies and Gentlemen*. Trans. Barbara Vedder. New York: Penguin, 1976.

Brombert, Victor. "Hugo, History and the Other Text." *Nineteenth Century French Studies*, 5 (1976-77), 23-33.

———. "Sentiment et violence chez Hugo, l'exemple de *Quatrevingt-Treize*." *Cahiers de l'Association Internationale des Etudes Françaises*, 24 (1974), 251-67.

Brunot, Ferdinand. *Histoire de la langue française des origines à 1900*. Vol. IX. Paris: Colin, 1937.

Buchez, Philippe-Joseph-Benjamin, and Prosper-Charles Roux. *Histoire parlementaire de la révolution française*. 40 vols. Paris: Paulin, 1834-38.

Camus, Albert. *The Myth of Sisyphus and Other Essays*. Trans. Justin O'Brien. New York: Vintage, 1960.

Carlyle, Thomas. *The French Revolution*. New York: Modern Library, 1934.

Dassal, Marcel. *Un Révolutionnaire jacobin, Charles Delescluze*. Paris: Marcel Rivière, 1952.

DeGeorge, Richard and Fernande, eds. *The Structuralists from Marx to Lévi-Strauss.* New York: Anchor, 1972.

Delfau, Gerard. "De la Terreur à la Commune: Jules Vallès, lecteur de *Quatrevingt-Treize.*" In *Les Ecrivains français devant la guerre de 1870 et devant la Commune.* Ed. Madeleine Fargeaud and Claude Pichois. Paris: Colin, 1972, pp. 137-52.

Empson, William. *Some Versions of Pastoral.* New York: New Directions, 1960.

Grant, Richard B. *The Perilous Quest: Image, Myth and Prophecy in the Narratives of Victor Hugo.* Durham: Duke University Press, 1968.

Hamilton, James F. "The Novelist as Historian: A Contrast between Balzac's *Les Chouans* and Hugo's *Quatrevingt-Treize.*" *French Review,* 49 (1975-76), 661-68.

Hugo, Victor. *Carnets intimes, 1870-1871.* Ed. Henri Guillemin. Paris: Gallimard, 1953.

———. *Œuvres complètes.* Ed. Jean Massin. Vols. XV and XVI. Paris: Club français du livre, 1970.

———. *Œuvres poétiques.* Ed. Pierre Albouy. Vol. III. Paris: Pléiade, 1974.

———. *Quatrevingt-Treize.* Ed. Jean Boudout. Paris: Garnier, 1963.

Johnson, Samuel. *Lives of the Poets: A Selection.* Ed. J. P. Hardy. Oxford: Clarendon, 1971.

Kristeva, Julia. *La Révolution du langage poétique.* Paris: Seuil, 1974.

Lévi-Strauss, Claude. *The Savage Mind.* Chicago: University of Chicago Press, 1966.

Lissagaray, Prosper. *Histoire de la Commune de 1871.* Paris: Librairie du Travail, 1929.

Lukács, Georg. *Studies in European Realism.* New York: Grosset and Dunlap, 1964.

Marinelli, Peter. *Pastoral.* London: Methuen, 1971.

Marx, Karl. *The Civil War in France.* Peking: Foreign Languages Press, 1970.

———. *The Eighteenth Brumaire of Louis Bonaparte.* New York: International Publishers, 1963.

Mehlman, Jeffrey. *Revolution and Repetition: Marx, Hugo, Balzac.* Berkeley: University of California Press, 1977.

Moussinac, Léon. *Eisenstein.* Trans. Sandy Petrey. New York: Crown, 1970.

Palmer, R. R., introd. *The Coming of the French Revolution.* By Georges Lefebvre. New York: Vintage, 1960.

Peyre, Henri. *Hugo.* Paris: Presses Universitaires de France, 1972.

Piroué, Georges. *Victor Hugo romancier, ou les dessus de l'inconnu*. Paris: Denoël, 1964.

Plato. *Selections*. Ed. Ralph Demos. New York: Scribners, 1955.

Pope, Alexander. *Pastoral Poetry and An Essay on Criticism*. Ed. E. Audra and A. Williams. New Haven: Yale Press, 1961.

Riffaterre, Michael. "L'Explication des faits littéraires." In *L'Enseignement de la littérature*. Ed. Serge Doubrovsky and Tzvetan Todorov. Paris: Plon, 1971, pp. 331-55.

————. "Interpretation and Descriptive Poetry: A Reading of Wordsworth's 'Yew-Trees.'" *New Literary History*, 4 (1972-73), 229-56.

Rosa, Guy. "Présentation de *Quatrevingt-Treize*." In Hugo, *Œuvres complètès*, XV, 229-60.

————. "*Quatrevingt-Treize* ou la critique du roman historique." *Revue d'histoire littéraire de la France*, 75 (1975), 329-43.

de Saussure, Ferdinand. *Course in General Linguistics*. Trans. Wade Baskin. New York: McGraw-Hill, 1959.

Soboul, Albert. *Les Sans-culottes parisiens de l'An II*. Paris: Clavreuil, 1958.

Thiers, Adolphe. *The History of the French Revolution*. Trans. Frederick Shoberl. London: Bentley, 1881. Vol. III.

Todorov, Tzvetan. *Introduction à la littérature fantastique*. Paris: Seuil, 1970.

Turton, Derek J. "Symbolic Confrontation in Hugo's *Quatrevingt-Treize*." *Revue de l'Université d'Ottawa*, 24 (1974), 373-83.

Vallès, Jules. *The Insurrectionist*. Trans. Sandy Petrey. Englewood Cliffs: Prentice-Hall, 1971.

Walter, Gérard. *La Révolution française*. Paris: Charpentier, 1967.

DATE DUE
